R. M McIntosh, H. R Christie, E. G Sewell

Words of Truth

a collection of hymns and tunes for Sunday schools and other occasions of Christian

work and worship

R. M McIntosh, H. R Christie, E. G Sewell

Words of Truth

a collection of hymns and tunes for Sunday schools and other occasions of Christian work and worship

ISBN/EAN: 9783337286620

Printed in Europe, USA, Canada, Australia, Japan

Cover: Foto ©Lupo / pixelio.de

More available books at **www.hansebooks.com**

WORDS OF TRUTH:

A COLLECTION

OF

HYMNS AND TUNES

FOR

SUNDAY-SCHOOLS

AND

OTHER OCCASIONS

OF

CHRISTIAN WORK AND WORSHIP.

EDITED BY

E. G. SEWELL AND R. M. McINTOSH.

ASSISTED BY

H. R. CHRISTIE.

NASHVILLE, TENN:
GOSPEL ADVOCATE PUBLISHING COMPANY.

[Copyright 1892, by GOSPEL ADVOCATE PUB. CO.]

PREFACE.

In presenting this volume to the public, we have endeavored to issue a book suited to the young. As the songs sung in childhood make the most lasting impression, it has been our aim to present nothing that would teach error.

We are sure that the utmost caution should be exercised in selecting songs for both old and young, especially the latter, as ideas gained in early life ar enduring.

With this aim before us we have sought to winnow the good out of the great mass from which we had to select, and give to the public only such songs as are scriptural in sentiment.

With all our pains to educate the youth in scriptural songs, we have not neglected those of maturer years. In this collection will be found many of the best standard hymns, the singing of which stirs every pure emotion of the heart in the old and the young alike.

Humbly praying God's richest blessings may attend it, and that the singing of these songs may help to ennoble and refine many, we leave it to those familiar with the word of God to judge how well we have succeeded.

. PUBLISHERS.

WORDS OF TRUTH.

No. 1. GOD SPEED THE RIGHT.

W. E. HIRKSON.  From the German.

1. { Now to heav'n our pray'rs as-cend-ing, God speed the right; }
   { In a no-ble cause con-tend-ing, God speed the right; }
2. { Be that pray'r a-gain re-peat-ed, God speed the right; }
   { Ne'er de-spair-ing though de-feat-ed, God speed the right; }

DUET.

Be our zeal in heav'n re-cord-ed, With suc-cess on
Like the good and great in sto-ry, If we fail, we

earth re-ward-ed, God speed the right, God speed the right.
fail with glo-ry, God speed the right, God speed the right.

3 Patient, firm, and persevering,
    God speed the right;
  Ne'er th'event nor danger fearing,
    God speed the right;
  Pains, nor toils, nor trials heeding,
  And in heaven's own time succeeding.
    ‖: God speed the right. :‖

4 Still our onward course pursuing,
    God speed the right;
  Every foe at length subduing,
    God speed the right;
  Truth our cause, whate'er delay it,
  There's no power on earth can stay it;
    ‖: God speed the right. :‖

No. 2. LITTLE PILGRIMS.

IDA L. REED.   FRANK M. DAVIS.

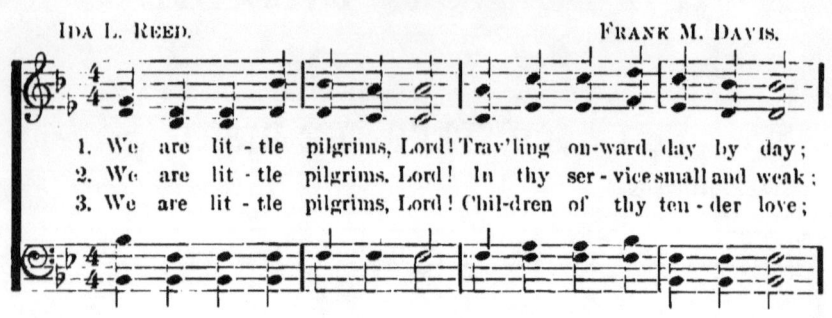

1. We are lit-tle pilgrims, Lord! Trav'ling on-ward, day by day;
2. We are lit-tle pilgrims, Lord! In thy ser-vice small and weak;
3. We are lit-tle pilgrims, Lord! Chil-dren of thy ten-der love;

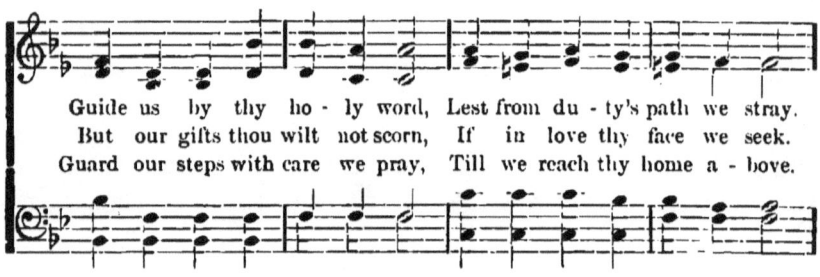

Guide us by thy ho-ly word, Lest from du-ty's path we stray.
But our gifts thou wilt not scorn, If in love thy face we seek.
Guard our steps with care we pray, Till we reach thy home a-bove.

CHORUS.

We are lit-tle pilgrims, Lord! O, be thou our dai-ly guide;

We will fol-low, we will trust; Keep us ev-er near thy side.

Copyright, 1892, by Gospel Advocate Pub. Co.

WHAT SHALL OUR RECORD BE? Concluded.

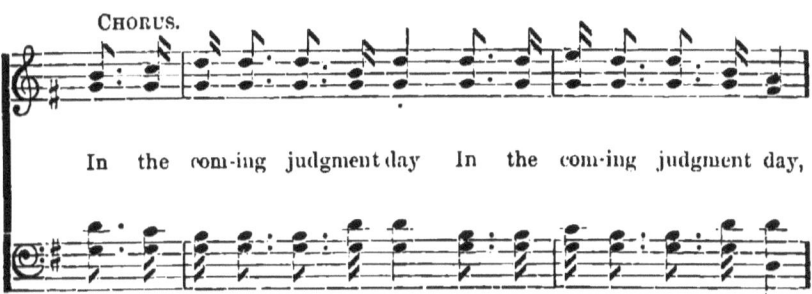

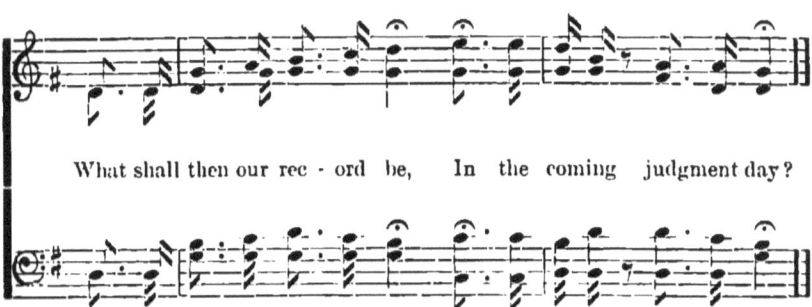

No. 8. HARK! THE HERALD ANGELS SING.

1. Hark! the her-ald an-gels sing Prais-es to the new-born king;
2. While the an-them rends the sky, Ju-dea's hills re-peat the cry—
3. All ye na-tions hail the birth Of the Sav-iour of the earth;

Peace on earth, good-will to men, Christ is born in Beth-le-hem.
Peace on earth, good-will to men, Christ is born in Beth-le-hem.
Shout his prais-es loud pro-claim, Christ is born in Beth-le-hem.

CHORUS.

Peace on earth, good-will to men, Christ is born in Beth-le-hem;

Rit - e - dem. ad lib.

Peace on earth, good-will to men; Peace, peace, peace on earth.

Copyright, 1892, by Gospel Advocate Pub. Co.

No. 9. WILL YOU COME?

C. H. G.

CHAS. H. GABRIEL.

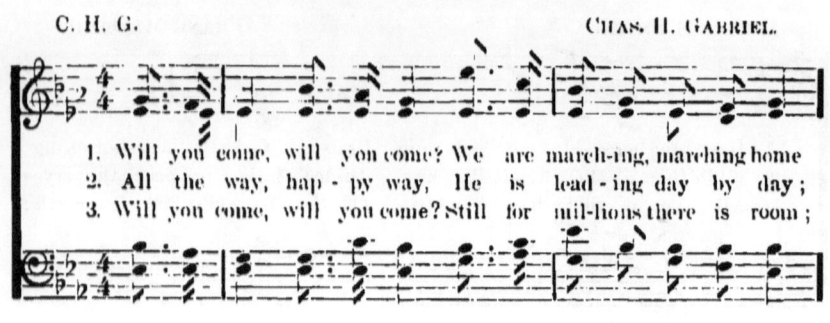

1. Will you come, will you come? We are march-ing, marching home
2. All the way, hap-py way, He is lead-ing day by day;
3. Will you come, will you come? Still for mil-lions there is room;

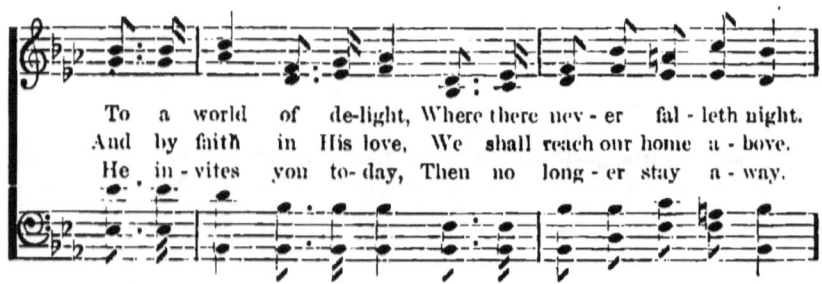

To a world of de-light, Where there nev-er fal-leth night.
And by faith in His love, We shall reach our home a-bove.
He in-vites you to-day, Then no long-er stay a-way.

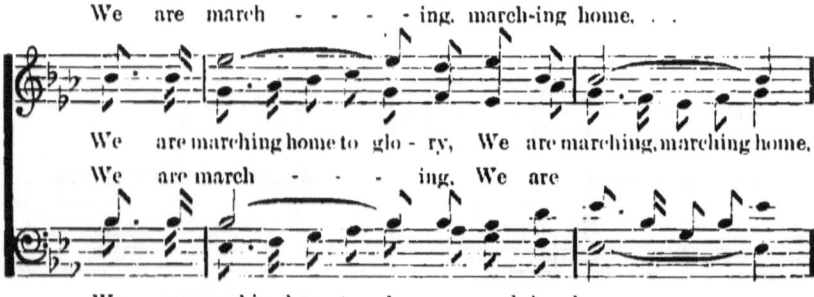

We are march - - - ing, march-ing home. . . .
We are marching home to glo-ry, We are marching, marching home.
We are march - - - ing, We are
We are marching home to glo-ry, march-ing home. . . . .

All for Je-sus is our song, As our way we press a-long,

Copyright, 1892, by Gospel Advocate Pub. Co.

WILL YOU COME? Concluded.

No. 10. ROSS. C. M.

Dr. A. B. Everett, by per.

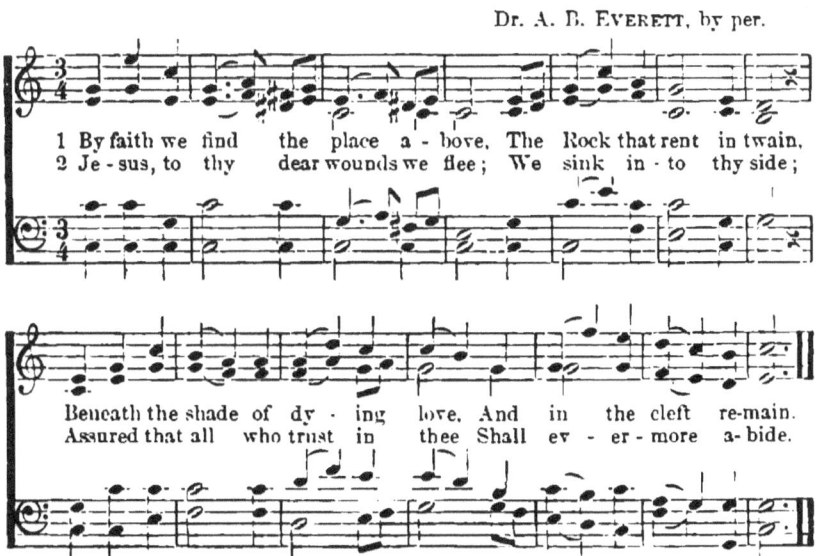

1 By faith we find the place a-bove, The Rock that rent in twain,
Beneath the shade of dy-ing love, And in the cleft re-main.

2 Je-sus, to thy dear wounds we flee; We sink in-to thy side;
Assured that all who trust in thee Shall ev-er-more a-bide.

UP TO THE WORK. Concluded.

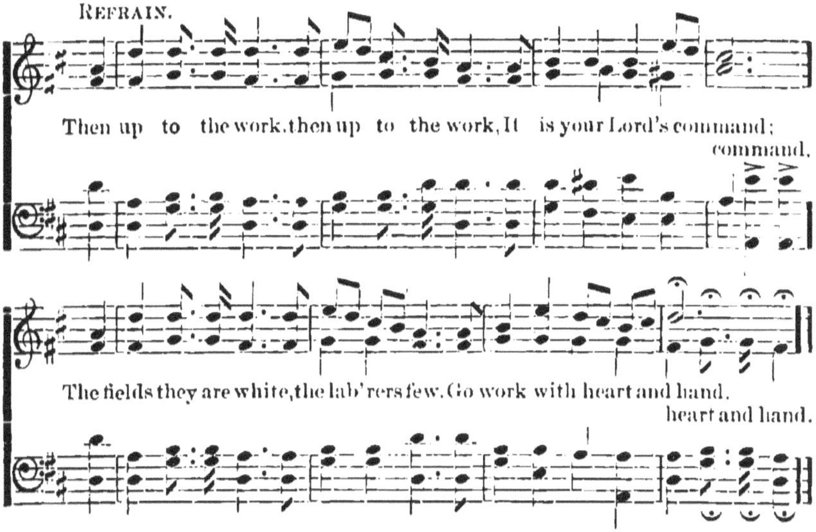

REFRAIN.

Then up to the work, then up to the work, It is your Lord's command;
command.

The fields they are white, the lab'rers few. Go work with heart and hand.
heart and hand.

No. 12. YARBROUGH.

Miss FRANCES E. HAVERGAL. Arr. by R. M. McINTOSH.

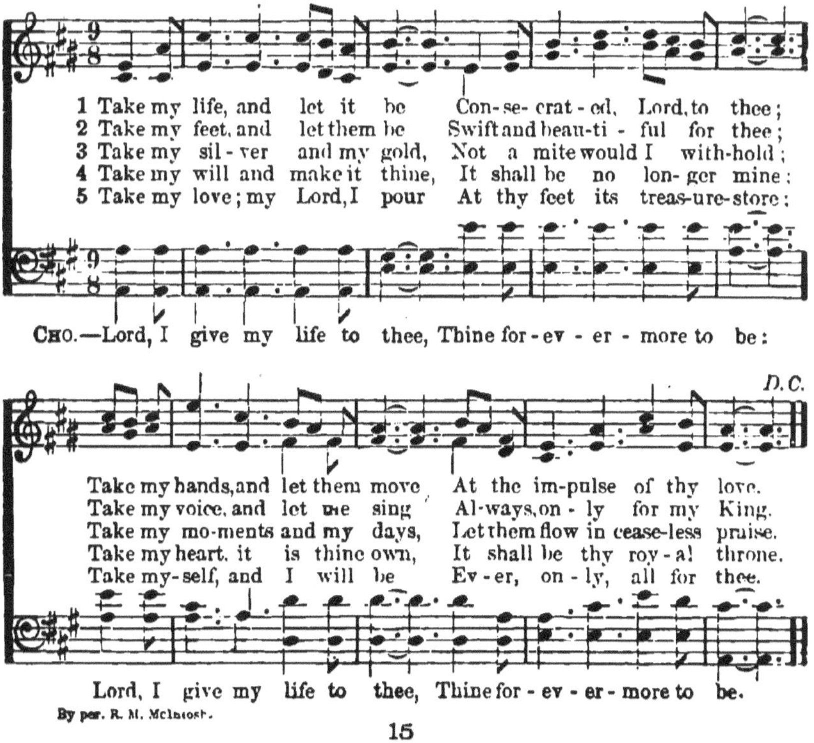

1 Take my life, and let it be Con-se-crat-ed, Lord, to thee;
2 Take my feet, and let them be Swift and beau-ti - ful for thee;
3 Take my sil - ver and my gold, Not a mite would I with-hold;
4 Take my will and make it thine, It shall be no lon-ger mine;
5 Take my love; my Lord, I pour At thy feet its treas-ure-store;

CHO.—Lord, I give my life to thee, Thine for-ev - er - more to be:

D.C.

Take my hands, and let them move At the im-pulse of thy love.
Take my voice, and let me sing Al-ways, on - ly for my King.
Take my mo-ments and my days, Let them flow in cease-less praise.
Take my heart, it is thine own, It shall be thy roy-al throne.
Take my-self, and I will be Ev - er, on - ly, all for thee.

Lord, I give my life to thee, Thine for - ev - er - more to be.

By per. R. M. McIntosh.

15

Would You go Home with the Angels? Concluded.

sin - ner; Think of your dread-ful end, Should
err - ing, And aid the help-less poor? Gen-tly

you die to-night. With-out the sin-ner's Friend
lead the chil-dren To seek a heaven-ly shore.

CHORUS.
Would you go home with the an-gels? Would you go home with the an-gels?
Ask him in faith. Je-sus will save; His life for you he gave.

No. 14. Shall We Know Each Other There.

Mrs. Annie E. Thomson. — Frank M. Davis.

1 When we've cross'd death's solemn river, When this troubled life is o'er,
2 Shall we meet our saint-ed mother, Who for ma-ny years hath slept,
3 Shall we see them robed in splendor, With no shad-ows on their brow,
4 He who soothes us in af-flictions, He whose love doth ne'er de-part,

And we go to dwell for-ev-er, Where the wea-ry weep no more;
Fa-ther, sis-ter dear, and brother, Whom we oft have mourn'd and wept?
Meet their lov-ing smiles so ten-der; Which our hearts are crav-ing now,
Breathes his heavenly ben-e-dictions, O'er each griev'd and wounded heart;

In those bright and heavenly pla-ces, Where the skies are al-ways fair,
Those un-to our hearts yet dear-er, Who our griefs were wont to share;
List to tones whose mu-sic on-ly Chased a-way each shade of care;
He who's left such bless-ed promise, Gives us bliss be-yond com-pare;

Shall we greet fa-mil-iar fa-ces? Shall we know each oth-er there?
In that fade-less light and clearer, Shall we know each oth-er there?
That have left the world so lone-ly, Shall we know each oth-er there?
He this joy will not take from us, We shall know each oth-er there.

Copyright, 1889, by R. M. McIntosh.

Shall We Know Each Other There. Concluded.

SONGS IN THE HEART. Concluded.

OH, TO BE THERE. Concluded.

No. 21. PAUL. S. M.

L. C. EVERETT. by per.

1 Je-sus, the Con-qu'ror, reigns, In glo-rious strength ar-rayed,
2 Ye sons of men, re-joice In Je-sus' might-y love;
3 Ex-tol his king-ly pow'r; Kiss the ex-alt-ed Son,
4 Our Ad-vo-cate with God, He un-der-takes our cause,

His kingdom o-ver all maintains, And bids the earth be glad!
Lift up your heart, lift up your voice, To him who rules a-bove.
Who died, and lives to die no more, High on his Fa-ther's throne;
And spreads thro' all the earth a-broad The vic-t'ry of his cross.

WE CALL THEE. Concluded.

No. 23. MANY MANSIONS.

F. E. BELDEN. FRANK M. DAVIS.

1. Ma - ny, ma - ny are the mansions Which our Sav - iour will pre-pare,
2. Yes, the dwell-ers all are ho - ly, In that cit - y of the pure,
3. When we leave this vale of sor - row, In that roy - al day of days;

Ma - ny, ma - ny are the chil-dren Who shall find a wel - come there;
And to such a - lone is giv - en This e - ter - nal prom - ise sure;
When we cease our toil and weeping, For e - ter - nal songs of praise;

But the dwell-ers all are ho - ly, Who the bless - ed prom - ise share.
O, the bless - ed hope of heav - en, From all earth - ly ills se - cure!
Then with-in those ma - ny mansions, That a - wait the pil-grims blest,

And their forms are like the an - gels That im-mor - tal ra diance wear.
How we long to see its glo - ry That un-fad - ing shall en - dure.
Shall we dwell at home for - ev - er, In that E - den land of rest?

Copyright, 1892, by Gospel Advocate Pub. Co.

30

MANY MANSIONS. Concluded.

Ma-ny man-sions, gold-en man-sions, Wait-ing, wait-ing for the blest,
In that cit-y robed with beauty, In that E-den land of rest.

No. 24. GILL. 8s, 7s, & 4s. (8th P. M.)

R. M. McIntosh, by per.

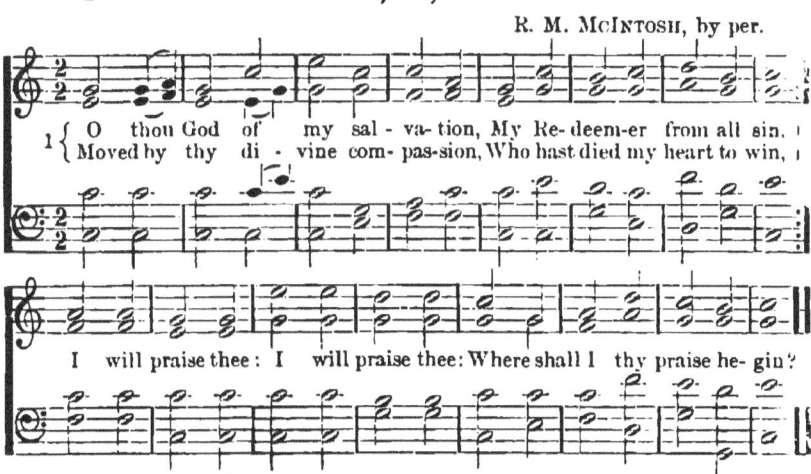

1 { O thou God of my sal-va-tion, My Re-deem-er from all sin,
   { Moved by thy di-vine com-pas-sion, Who hast died my heart to win,
I will praise thee: I will praise thee: Where shall I thy praise be-gin?

2 Though unseen, I love the Saviour:
   He hath brought salvation near—
   Manifests his pardoning favor,
   And, when Jesus doth appear,
   Soul and body
   Shall his glorious image bear.

3 While the angel choirs are crying,
   Glory to the great I AM!
   I with them will still be vying,
   Glory! glory to the Lamb!
   O how precious
   Is the sound of Jesus' name!

4 Angels now are hovering round us,
   Unperceived they mix the throng,
   Wondering at the love that crowned us,
   Glad to join the holy song:
   Hallelujah!
   Love and praise to Christ belong!

No. 27. MY HERITAGE IN HEAVEN.

IDA L. REED.   FRANK M. DAVIS.

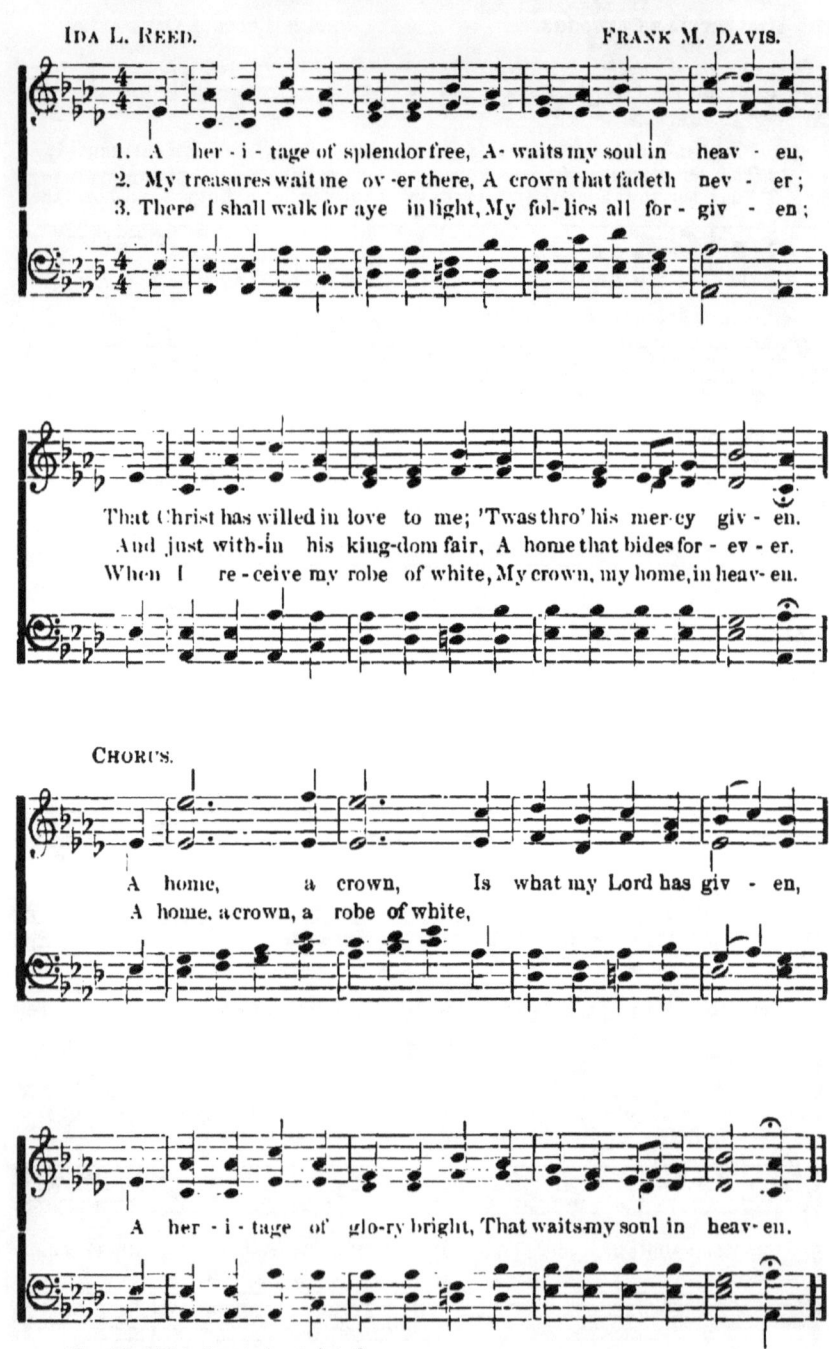

1. A her-i-tage of splendor free, A-waits my soul in heav-en,
2. My treasures wait me ov-er there, A crown that fadeth nev-er;
3. There I shall walk for aye in light, My fol-lies all for-giv-en;

That Christ has willed in love to me; 'Twas thro' his mer-cy giv-en.
And just with-in his king-dom fair, A home that bides for-ev-er.
When I re-ceive my robe of white, My crown, my home, in heav-en.

CHORUS.

A home, a crown, Is what my Lord has giv-en,
A home, a crown, a robe of white,

A her-i-tage of glo-ry bright, That waits my soul in heav-en.

Copyright, 1892, by Gospel Advocate Pub. Co.

No. 28. CHILDREN OF JERUSALEM.

Arr. by R. M. McIntosh.

1 Chil-dren of Je - ru - sa - lem, Sang the praise of Je-sus' name:
2 We have oft - en heard and read What the roy - al psalm-ist said:
3 We are taught to love the Lord, We are taught to read his word,
4 Par-ents, teach-ers, old and young, All u - nite to swell the song:

Chil - dren, too, of lat - er days, Join to sing the Saviour's praise.
Babes and sucklings' art - less lays Shall pro - claim the Saviour's praise.
We are taught the way to heav'n, Praise to God for all be given.
High - er and yet high-er rise, Till ho - san - nas reach the skies.

REFRAIN.

Hark! Hark! Hark! while in - fant voi - ces sing, Hark! Hark!

Hark! while in - fant voi - ces sing Loud ho - san - nas,

Loud ho - san - nas, Loud ho - san - nas to our King.

Copyright, 1889, by R. M. McIntosh.

BE CONTENT WITH YOUR LOT. Concluded.

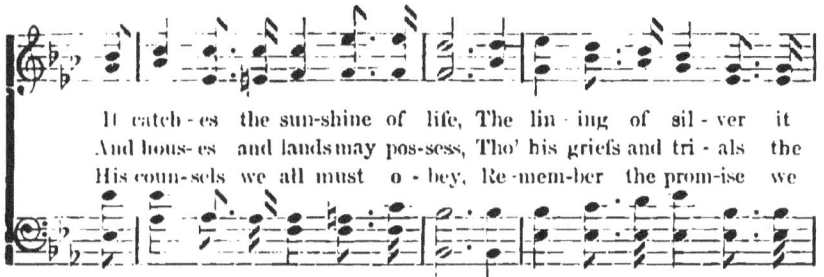

It catch-es the sun-shine of life, The lin-ing of sil-ver it
And hous-es and lands may pos-sess, Tho' his griefs and tri-als the
His coun-sels we all must o-bey, Re-mem-ber the prom-ise we

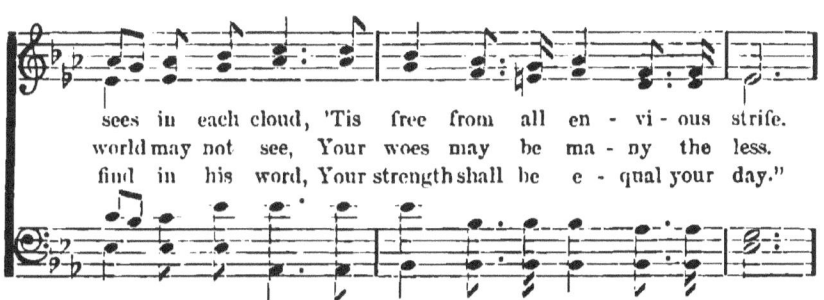

sees in each cloud, 'Tis free from all en-vi-ous strife.
world may not see, Your woes may be ma-ny the less.
find in his word, Your strength shall be e-qual your day."

REFRAIN.

Be content, with your lot, Tho' hum-ble it may be,
Be content, with your lot.

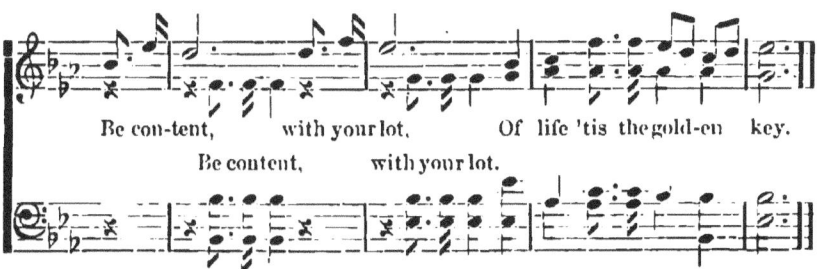

Be con-tent, with your lot, Of life 'tis the gold-en key.
Be content, with your lot.

OVER THE SILENT SEA. Concluded.

No. 31. DUNCAN. S. M.

R. M. McIntosh, by per.

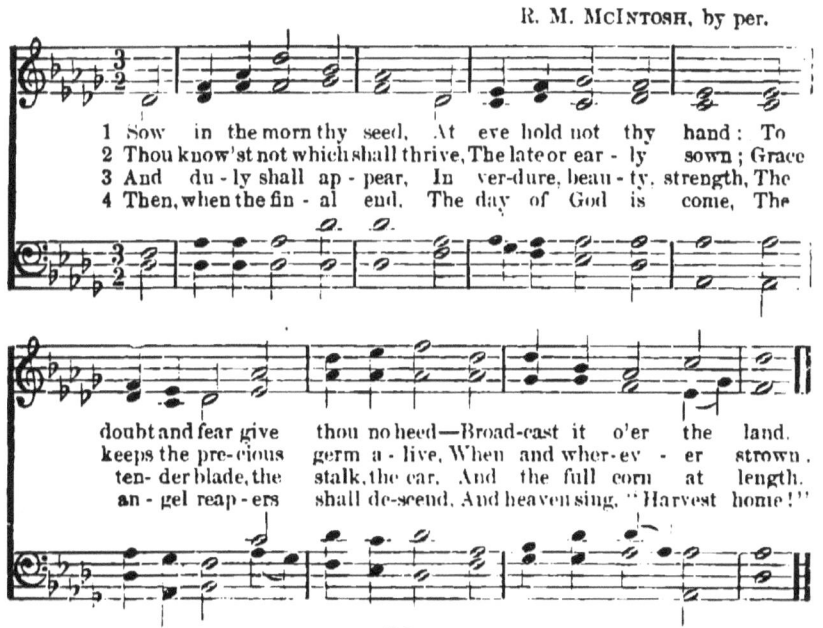

PARTING HYMN. Concluded.

Soon we'll meet, no more to sev - er, In the home of cloudless light.
We shall meet to live

No. 33. GREGORY.

L. C. EVERETT, by per.

1 Be it my on - ly wis-dom here To serve the Lord with fil - ial fear,
2 O may I still from sin de - part; A wise and un - derstanding heart,

With lov - ing grat - i - tude; Su - pe - rior sense may I dis-play,
Je - sus, to me be giv'n! And let me thro' thy spir - it know

By shunning ev - 'ry e - vil way, And walk - ing in the good.
To glo - ri - fy my God be-low, And find my way to heav'n.

No. 36. HALLELUJAH.

HALLELUJAH. Concluded.

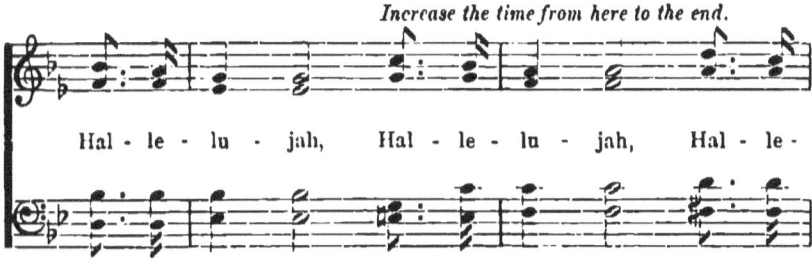

I WALK NOT ALONE. Concluded.

ONWARD WE'RE MARCHING. Concluded.

path - way; Un - der the Sav - iour's com - mand.

No. 41. JESUS IS MINE.

R. M. McIntosh, by per.

1 Fade, fade each earthly joy, Je - sus is mine; Break ev - 'ry ten-der tie,
2 Tempt not my soul a - way, Je - sus is mine; Here would I ev - er stay,
3 Farewell, ye dreams of night, Je - sus is mine; Lost in this dawning light,
4 Farewell, mor - tal - i - ty, Je - sus is mine; Welcome e - ter - ni - ty.

Je - sus is mine; Dark is the wil - der-ness, Earth has no
Je - sus is mine; Per - ish - ing things of clay, Born but for
Je - sus is mine; All that my soul has tried, Left but a
Je - sus is mine; Wel-come, O loved and blest, Welcome, sweet

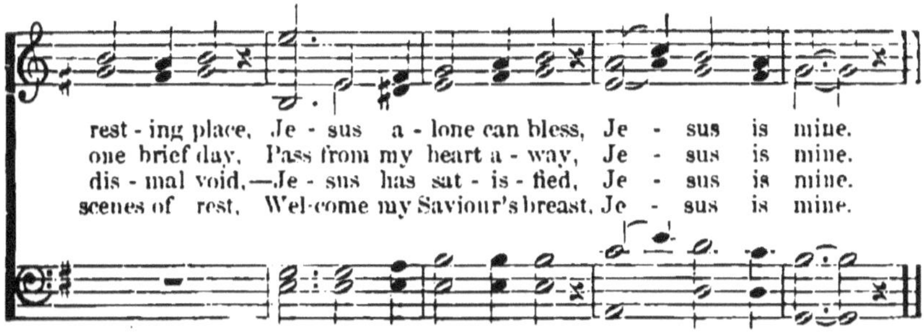

rest - ing place, Je - sus a - lone can bless, Je - sus is mine.
one brief day, Pass from my heart a - way, Je - sus is mine.
dis - mal void,—Je - sus has sat - is - fied, Je - sus is mine.
scenes of rest, Wel-come my Saviour's breast, Je - sus is mine.

WE ARE COMING. Concluded.

No. 43. GEORGIA. S. M.

R. M. McIntosh, by per.

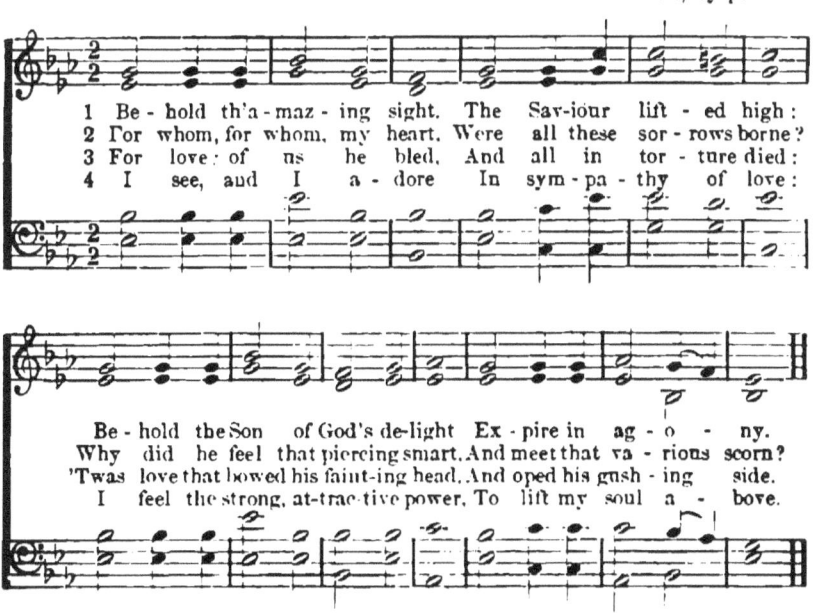

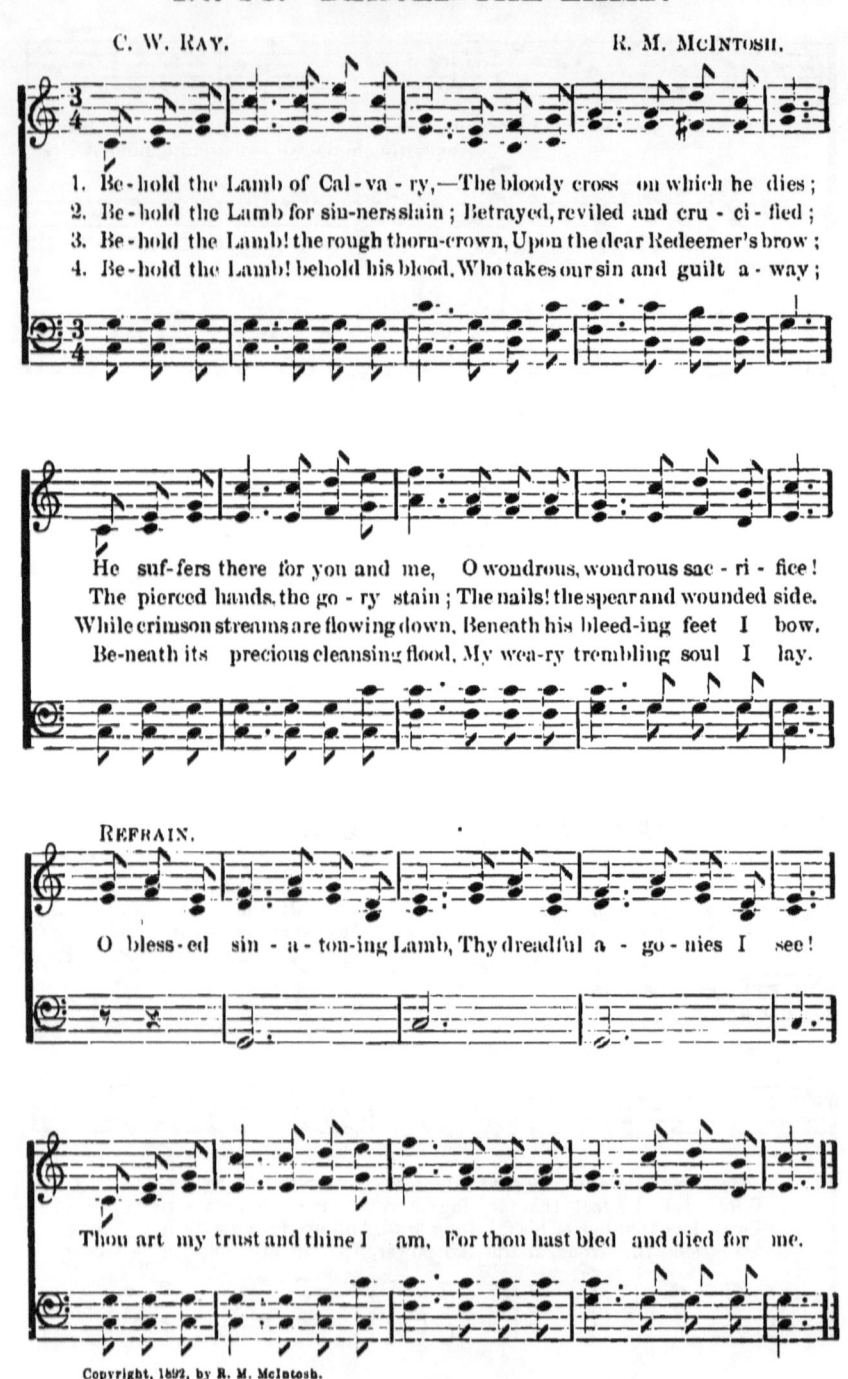

No. 45. HE CALLETH ME HOME.

ELISHA A. HOFFMAN.   JOHN M. RICHARDSON.

1. Though far from the fold of the Sav-iour, In sin and
2. In tears I have oft-en la-ment-ed The sins that
3. Was ev-er a voice so en-dear-ing? Was e'er af-
4. To-night with my soul he is plead-ing And kind-ly
   (To-day)

fol-ly I roam; Yet ev-er I hear a sweet whisper That
led me a-stray; The call of the Lord was so ten-der, I
fec-tion so true? How can I then long-er re-sist him? Oh!
bids me to come; A-gain his sweet voice in-ter-ced-ing En-

CHORUS.

ten-der-ly call-eth me home. ⎫ Come home, come home, come
scarce from his pres-ence could stay. ⎬
what in my woe shall I do? ⎪
treats me, "O wand'rer, come home!" ⎭ Come home, come home,

home, ... For-ev-er he call-eth me home.
come home, come home.

Copyright, 1892, by R. M. McIntosh.

No. 46. IN OUR FATHER'S HOUSE.

C. W. Ray. R. M. McIntosh.

1. In our Father's house, There are mansions bright and fair, And we'll soon be at home over there; With our Saviour King, Who his sanc-ti-fied will bring, The de-lights of his king-dom to share.
2. In our Father's house, All the faith-ful shall be crown'd, While the an-thems of wel-come re-sound; We shall then be-hold How the wand-'rer from the fold, By the Sav-iour was sought and was found.
3. In our Father's house There's a her-i-tage for all, Where the shad-ows of night nev-er fall; Where, thro' end-less years, Neith-er cares, nor griefs, nor fears, Shall the ran-somed of Je-sus en-thrall.

REFRAIN.

We shall rest, ... with the blest, In our
    We shall rest,   with the blest,
heav'nly Father's house a-bove; We shall rest, ... for-ev-er—
                                     We shall rest.

Copyright, 1892, by R. M. McIntosh.

IN OUR FATHER'S HOUSE. Concluded.

more, In the bos-om of our Sav-iour's love.
for-ev-ermore.

No. 47. RICHMOND. S. M. Double.

Dr. A. B. EVERETT, by per.

1 A charge to keep I have, A God to glo-ri-fy;
2 Arm me with jeal-ous care, As in thy sight to live:

A nev-er-dy-ing-soul to save, And fit it for the sky;
And O, thy ser-vant, Lord, pre-pare A strict ac-count to give!

D.S.—O may it all my powers en-gage To do my Mas-ter's will!
As-sured if I my trust be-tray, I shall for-ev-er die.

To serve the pres-ent age, My call-ing to ful-fil:
Help me to watch and pray, And on thy-self re-ly,

No. 48. JESUS A TRUE FRIEND.

E. A. H.
Elisha A. Hoffman.

1. How kind a friend is Je - sus! He loves me ten - der - ly,
2. He is the friend of sin - ners, And shed his pre - cious blood
3. A help - er to the help - less, A com - fort - er is he;

And walks with me each mo - ment, My guard and guide to be!
That they might be for - giv - en, And rec - on - ciled to God;
He, in the time of trou - ble, A tower of strength will be;

How ma - ny are the bless-ings Be-stowed up - on his child.
All who in faith obey him Re - ceive a par - don free.
And when the world as - sails thee, Trust thou his might - y arm

To shield me from all e - vil, And keep me un - de - filed!
And if thy soul can trust him, Thy Sav - iour he will be.
To suc - cor and de - fend thee, And keep thy soul from harm.

Copyright, 1892, by Gospel Advocate Pub. Co.

JESUS A TRUE FRIEND. Concluded.

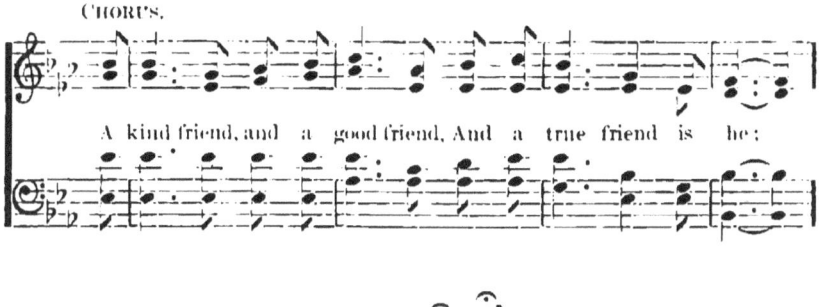

No. 49. VIRGINIA. C. M.

N. E. EVERETT, by per.

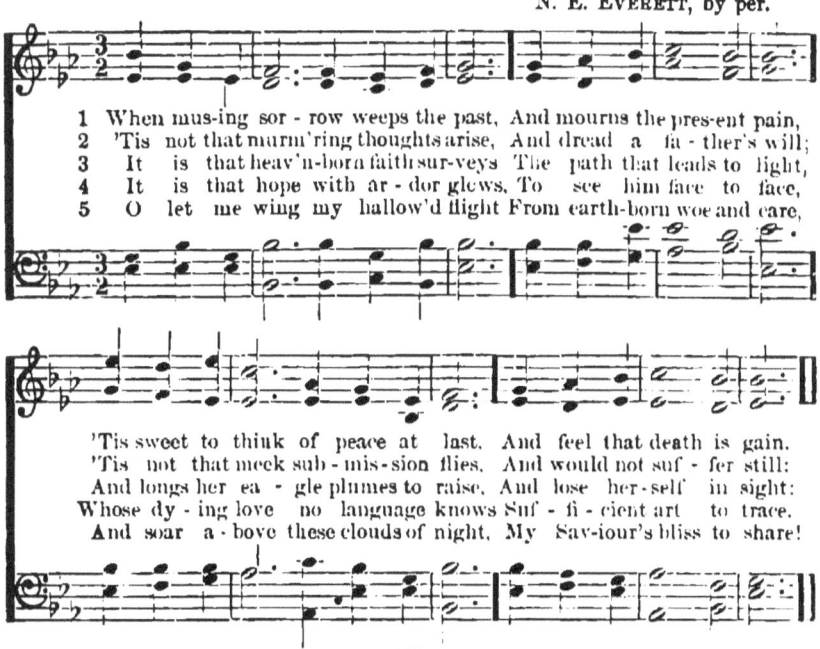

1 When mus-ing sor - row weeps the past, And mourns the pres-ent pain,
2 'Tis not that murm'ring thoughts arise, And dread a fa - ther's will;
3 It is that heav'n-born faith sur-veys The path that leads to light,
4 It is that hope with ar - dor glows, To see him face to face,
5 O let me wing my hallow'd flight From earth-born woe and care,

'Tis sweet to think of peace at last, And feel that death is gain.
'Tis not that meek sub - mis - sion flies, And would not suf - fer still:
And longs her ea - gle plumes to raise, And lose her-self in sight:
Whose dy - ing love no language knows Suf - fi - cient art to trace.
And soar a - bove these clouds of night, My Sav-iour's bliss to share!

No. 51. FATHER OF LOVE.

ELISHA A. HOFFMAN. R. M. McINTOSH.

1. Fa - ther of love, in heav'n a- bove, Re - gard our fer - vent plea;
2. Draw ver - y near, O, Sav- iour dear! And fill this hal- low'd place:
3. O, Father blest! afford us rest, And sanc - ti - fy each heart;

Our fears re-lieve, our sins forgive, And seal our hearts to thee.
And on us pour, in bounteous store, The blessings of thy grace.
Forgive us now, as here we bow, And per- fect peace im - part.

REFRAIN.

O, take a- way our guilt and shame, In Je- sus' all - pre-vail- ing name!

Oh, take a- way our guilt and shame, And seal us thine e - ter- nal- ly.

Copyright, 1892, by R. M. McIntosh.

WE PRAISE HIM. Concluded.

No. 53. THE LAMB OF CALVARY.

J. H. MARTIN.   R. M. McINTOSH, by per.

1 There was love, deep love, in the cross dis-played, When the Lamb of Cal-va-ry died, For the lost in sin was sac-ri-fice made, When the Lamb of Cal-va-ry died.

2 There is love, strong love, in the King on high To the souls condemned for their guilt, He will save the lost that to him draw nigh Thro' the pre-cious blood that he spilt.

3 There is love, warm love, in the Sav-iour's heart For the troub-led, wretched, and weak; In his bound-less grace he will peace im-part To the mourn-er, low-ly and meek.

4 Un-to Je-sus come with your load of grief, And re-pose by faith on his breast, There your bur-dened spir-it shall find re-lief— On the Lamb of Cal-va-ry rest.

REFRAIN.

'Twas a bless-ed, bless-ed day for our wretch-ed race

Copyright, 1885, by R. M. McIntosh.

THE LAMB OF CALVARY. Concluded.

No. 54. There's A Call for Willing Workers.

F. M. D.
Frank M. Davis.

1. There's a call for the will-ing work-ers, The tide of de-struct-ion to stay; Hear the voice of the Mas-ter say-ing, "Go work in my vineyard to-day."
2. There's a call for the will-ing work-ers, The fields of the har-vest are white; There are souls, prec-ious souls to gath-er, Ere fall-eth the shad-ows of night.
3. There's a call for the will-ing work-ers, To glean in the high-ways of sin, Go-ing forth with a firm en-deav-or, To gath-er the wan-der-ers in.

CHORUS.

Go work, go work, Go work in my vine-yard to-day; to-day. Hear the voice of the Mas-ter say-ing, "Go work in my vine-yard to-day."

Copyright, 1892, by R. M. McIntosh.

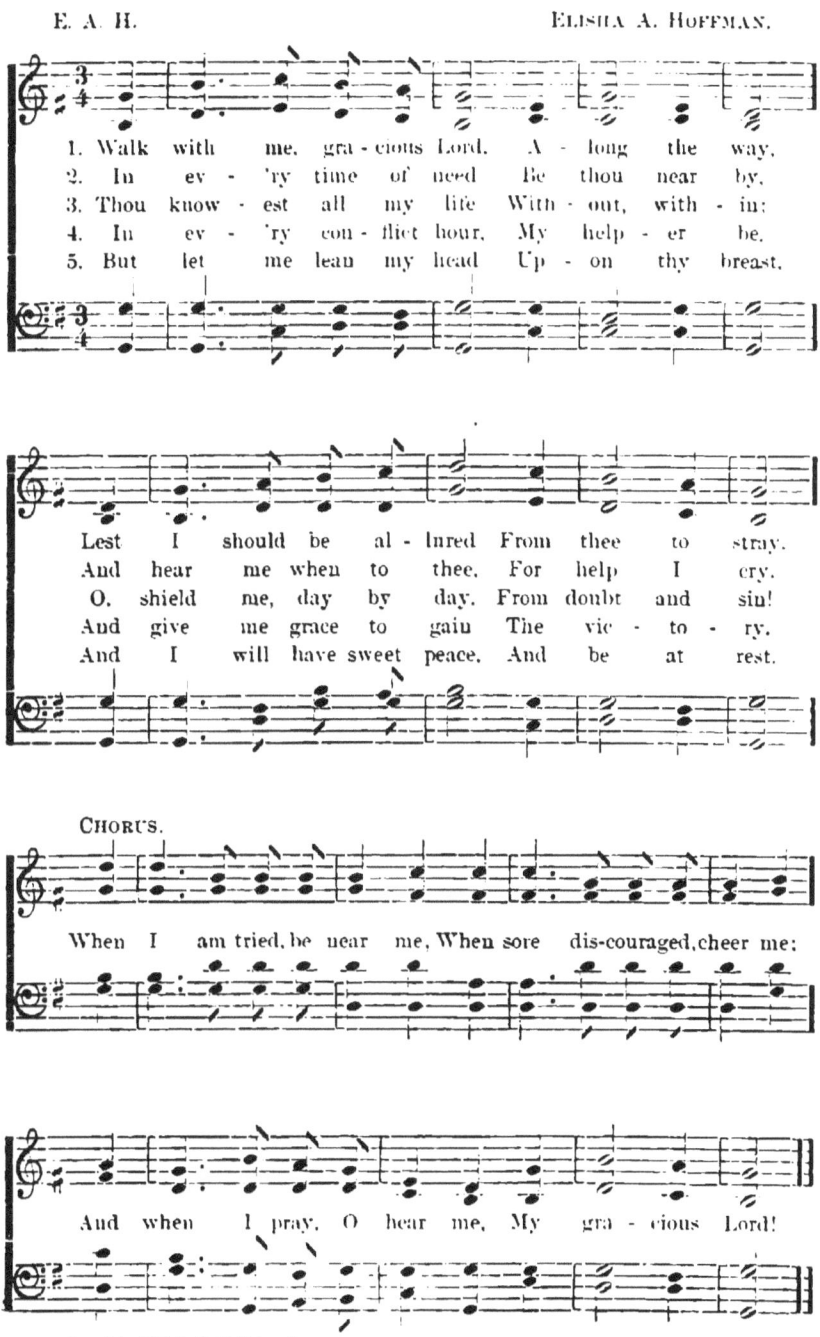

I'LL BE THERE. Concluded.

No. 57. SITTING AT THE FEET OF JESUS.

Anon.   A. J. SHOWALTER.

1. Sit-ting at the feet of Jesus, O what words I hear him say!(hear him say!)
2. Sit-ting at the feet of Jesus, Where could mortal be more blest?(be more blest?)
3. Bless me, O my Saviour, bless me, As I sit low at thy feet!(at thy feet!)

Hap-py place, so near, so pre-cious! May it find me there each day!
There I lay my sins and sor-rows, And when wea-ry, find sweet rest.
Oh, look down in love up-on me, Let me see thy face so sweet!

Sit-ting at the feet of Je-sus, I would look up-on the past;
Sit-ting at the feet of Je-sus, There I love to weep and pray.
Give me Lord, the mind of Je-sus, Make me ho-ly as he is:

For his love has been so pre-cious, It has won my heart at last.
While I from his ful-ness gath-er Grace and com-fort day by day.
May I prove I've been with Je-sus, Who is all my right-cous-ness!

Copyright, 1892, by A. J. Showalter.

No. 58. WHEN THE HARVEST ALL IS IN.

E. R. LATTA. FRANK M. DAVIS.

1. Would you stand a-mong the toil-ers, When the har-vest all is in?
2. Would you join the song of gladness, When the har-vest all is in?
3. Would you have some sheaves to of-fer, When the har-vest all is in?
4. Would you have a crown e-ter-nal, When the har-vest all is in?

For the bless-ed Lord and Mas-ter, You must here the work be-gin.
You must be a faith-ful glean-er In the haunts of woe and sin.
From the husks of want and fol-ly, Strive the prod-i-gals to win.
Seek to swell the heav'nly gar-ner, Ere it be too late to glean.

CHORUS.

When the har-vest all is in, When the har-vest all is in,
What a meet-ing of the reap-ers, What a shout-ing of ho-san-nas, When the harv-est all is in.

Copyright, 1892, by R. M. McIntosh.

No. 60. COME TO-DAY.

Mrs. LAURA E. NEWELL.   A. J. SHOWALTER.

1. Hear the Sav-iour's in - vi - ta - tion, "Come to me to - day;"
2. Hear the Sav-iour's in - vi - ta - tion; Seek the heav'nly fold;
3. Free sal-va-tion now he of - fers, Seek the heav'nly fold;
4. Come to-day, no oth - er ref - uge E'er may mor-tals know;
5. He has died your soul to res - cue; None may love as he;

All ye peo-ple, ev - 'ry na - tion, Heark-en and o - bey.
All ye peo-ple, ev - 'ry na - tion, En - ter young and old.
While he kind - ly bids you en - ter, Ere your hearts grow cold.
Lis - ten to his ten - der pleading; He would bear your woe.
Come to Je - sus, he is call-ing, Call - ing ten - der - ly.

REFRAIN.

Come to - day, come to-day, While he is sweet-ly call - ing;

On your ear, soft and clear His lov - ing tones are fall - ing.

Copyright, 1892, by A. J. Showalter.

ON THE WAY TO HEAVEN. Concluded.

No. 62. BLESS US AND KEEP US.

JULIA H. JOHNSTON. FRANK M. DAVIS.

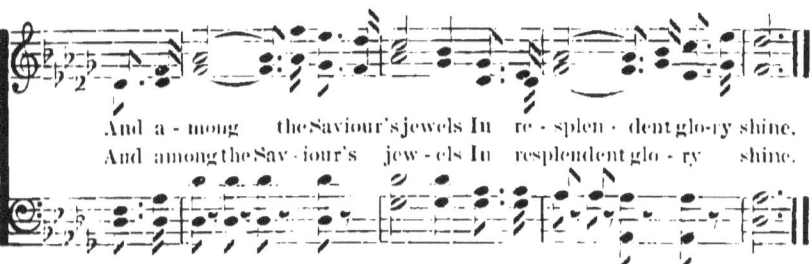

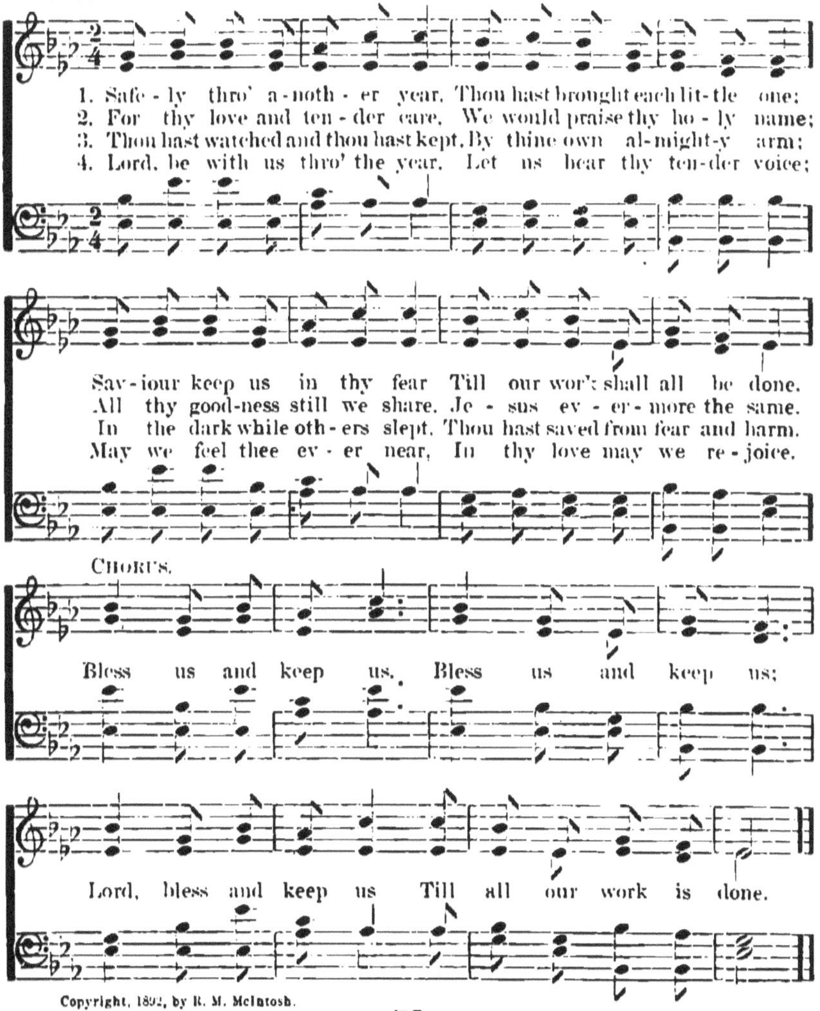

Copyright, 1892, by R. M. McIntosh.

No. 63. THE HALF HE HAS NEVER REVEALED.

ELISHA A. HOFFMAN. R. M. McINTOSH.

1. The half he has nev-er re-vealed Of all his af-fec-tion for me;
2. The half he has nev-er re-vealed Of all the compassion and grace,
3. The half he has nev-er re-vealed Of all the rich treasures of peace.
4. The half he has nev-er re-vealed Of all the pure rapture and bliss

Each day doth more ful-ly un-fold His love, so a-maz-ing and free.
That led him to Cal-va-ry's cross, To die for the poor sinner's sake.
He holds in re-serve for my soul The stores of its wealth to increase.
He waits on my soul to be-stow; What wondrous redemption is this!

REFRAIN.

And this is his prom-ise so sweet, My per-fect Redeemer to be,

Each day his a-dor-a-ble love More ful-ly reveal-ing in me.

Copyright, 1892, by R. M. McIntosh.

No. 65. LAMP OF OUR FEET.

BARTON, arr.   A. J. SHOWALTER.

1. Lamp of our feet! by thee we trace Our path when wont to stray;
2. Bread of our souls whereon we feed, True manna from on high;
3. Word of the ev-er-last-ing God, The gos-pel of his Son;
4. Help us, O Lord, a-right to learn The wis-dom it im-parts,

Thou art the stream of heav'nly grace, The brook be-side our way.
Our guide and chart, where-in we read Of realms be-yond the sky.
With-out thee how could earth be trod, Or how could heav'n be won?
And to its heav'n-ly teach-ing turn, With sim-ple, child like hearts.

REFRAIN.

Our Lamp, our guide, the light of our path, Our an-chor and our stay;
A pil-lar of fire thro' watches dark, A ra-diant cloud by day.

Copyright, 1892, by A. J. Showalter.

A LITTLE LONGER LABOR ON. Concluded.

CHORUS.

The crown,... the crown,... To us will then be giv-en,
The gold-en crown, the shin-ing crown,

The crown,... the crown,... When we ar-rive in heav'n.
The gold-en crown, the shin-ing crown,

No. 68. ST. THOMAS. S. M.

WM. HAMMOND.

1. A-wake, and sing the song Of Mo - ses and the Lamb;
2. Sing of his dy - ing love; Sing of his ris - ing power;
3. Sing on your heav'n-ly way. You ran - somed sin - ners, sing;
4. Soon shall you hear him say, "You bless - ed children come!"

Wake, ev - 'ry heart and ev - 'ry tongue, To praise the Saviour's name.
Sing how he in - ter-cedes a - bove For those whose sins he bore.
Sing on, re - joic - ing ev - 'ry day In Christ, the glo - rious King.
Soon will he call you hence a - way, And take his pil-grims home.

No. 69. TEMPTED AND TRIED.

C. W. Ray. R. M. McIntosh.

1. Art thou tempt-ed and tried? In thy Sav-iour con-fide, Tho' a-round thee the bil-lows may roll; He who stooped on the wave Sink-ing Pe-ter to save, He will shel-ter and care for thy soul.
2. Art thou tempt-ed and tried? Still in Je-sus a-bide, He shall rule both the wind and the sea; He will van-quish thy foes, He will ban-ish thy woes, And his bo-som thy ref-uge shall be.
3. Art thou tempt-ed and tried? Then whatev-er be-tide, Trust in Je-sus whose arm can-not fail; If his fa-vor be thine, Tho' all worlds may com-bine, Naught a-gainst thee shall ev-er pre-vail.

REFRAIN.

He who walked on the wave Is al-might-y to save; Trust thy soul to his mer-cy and care; Then in in-fi-nite love He shall

Copyright, 1892, by R. M. McIntosh.

TEMPTED AND TRIED. Concluded.

bring thee a-bove, All the wealth of his glo-ry to share.

No. 70.   JESUS IN GETHSEMANE.

H. S.
H. SANDERS.

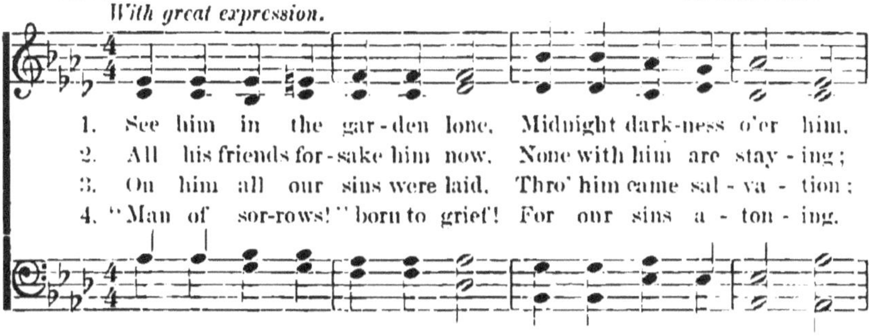

With great expression.

1. See him in the gar-den lone, Midnight dark-ness o'er him.
2. All his friends for-sake him now, None with him are stay-ing;
3. On him all our sins were laid, Thro' him came sal-va-tion;
4. "Man of sor-rows!" born to grief! For our sins a-ton-ing.

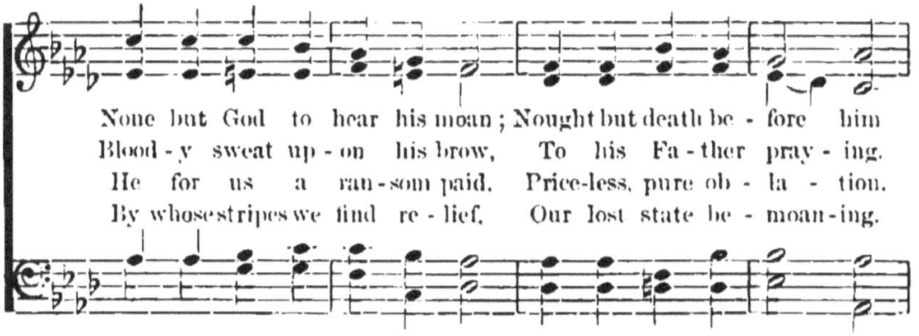

None but God to hear his moan; Nought but death be-fore him
Blood-y sweat up-on his brow, To his Fa-ther pray-ing.
He for us a ran-som paid, Price-less, pure ob-la-tion.
By whose stripes we find re-lief, Our lost state be-moan-ing.

All a-lone! all a-lone! He the wine-press treads a-lone.
All a-lone! all a-lone! He the wine-press treads a-lone.
All a-lone! all a-lone! He the wine-press trod a-lone.
All a-lone! all a-lone! He the wine-press trod a-lone.

Copyright, 1892, by R. M. McIntosh.

THEY SHALL SHINE. Concluded.

With a rap-ture un-told, O'er the pave-ments of gold, Arm in

arm with ho-ly an-gels,They shall walk in sweet ac - cord.

No. 72. BONNELL. C. M.

R. M. McIntosh, by per.

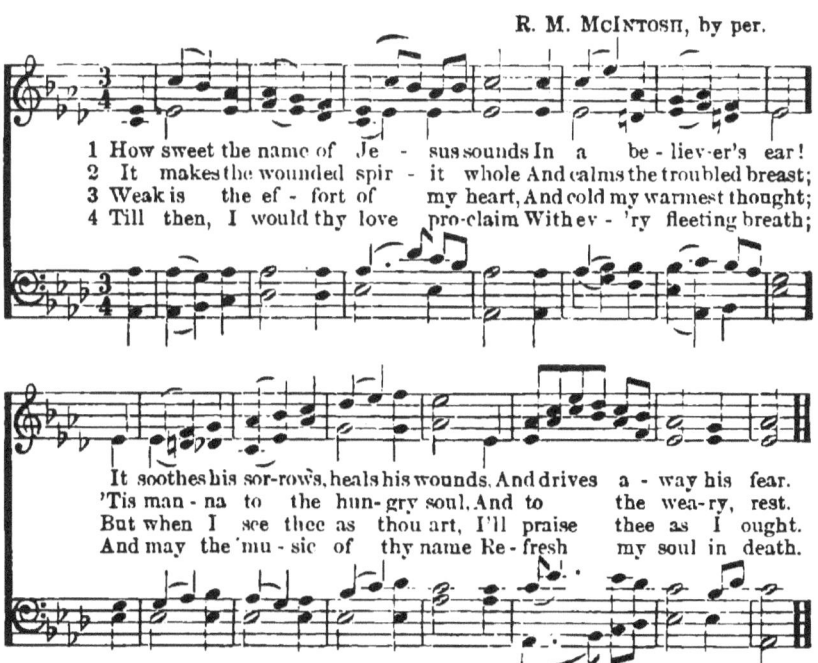

1 How sweet the name of Je - sus sounds In a be - liev-er's ear!
2 It makes the wounded spir - it whole And calms the troubled breast;
3 Weak is the ef - fort of my heart, And cold my warmest thought;
4 Till then, I would thy love pro-claim With ev - 'ry fleeting breath;

It soothes his sor-rows, heals his wounds, And drives a - way his fear.
'Tis man - na to the hun-gry soul, And to the wea-ry, rest.
But when I see thee as thou art, I'll praise thee as I ought.
And may the 'mu - sic of thy name Re - fresh my soul in death.

No. 74. TAKE YOUR HARPS.

ALEXCENAH THOMAS. W. A. OGDEN.

1. Take your harps on wil-lows hung, Sound them forth in joy-ful lays,
2. Take your harps, oh pil-grim band, Weep no more by Babylon's wave,
3. Take your harps, and tune each string To the song the an-gels sang;

Let the Saviour's name be sung In a song of loft-y praise.
Shout the tid-ings thro' the land, Je-sus Christ is strong to save.
Let the Saviour's praises ring As the heav-enly cho-rus rang.

CHORUS.

Swell the joy-ful an-them, high Un-to God your voic-es raise;

With the ho-ly an-gels vie, In a might-y song of praise.

Copyright, 1892, by W. A. Ogden.

BE OF GOOD COURAGE. Concluded.

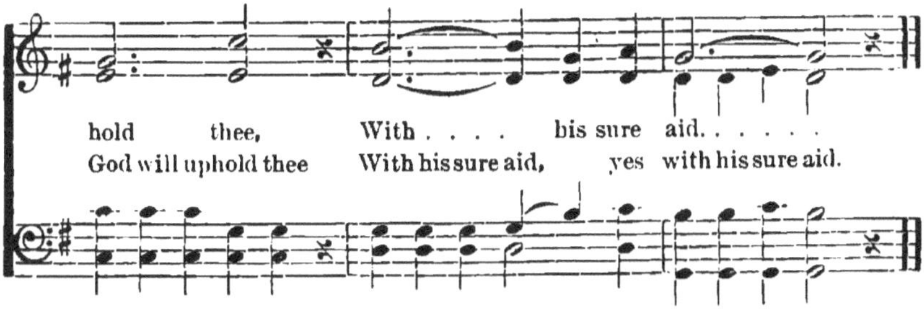

hold thee, With .... bis sure aid......
God will uphold thee With his sure aid, yes with his sure aid.

No. 76. ANTIOCH. C. M.

1 Joy to the world, the Lord is come! Let earth re-ceive her King;
2 Joy to the earth, the Sav-iour reigns! Let men their songs em-ploy;

Let ev-'ry heart pre-pare him room, And heav'n and na-ture sing.
While fields and floods, rocks, hill, and plains, Re-peat the sounding joy.

And heav'n and na-
Re-peat the sound-

And heav'n and na-ture sing, And heav'n, and heav'n and na-ture sing.
Re-peat the sounding joy, Re-peat, re-peat the sounding joy.
-ture sing, ...
-ing joy, ...

-ture sing, And heav'n and nature sing, And heav'n and na-ture sing.
-ing joy, Re-peat the sounding joy, Re-peat the sound-ing joy.

3 No more let sins and sorrows grow,
   Nor thorns infest the ground:
   He comes to make his blessings flow,
   Far as the curse is found.

4 He rules the world with truth and grace;
   And makes the nations prove
   The glories of his righteousness,
   And wonders of his love.

THE CHILDREN FOR JESUS. Concluded.

Lead-ing the dear lit-tle chil-dren to thee; The dear little children whom thou wilt fondly own, In glo-ry e-ter-nal, up-on thy throne.

No. 78. DAVIES. 7s.

R. M. McIntosh.

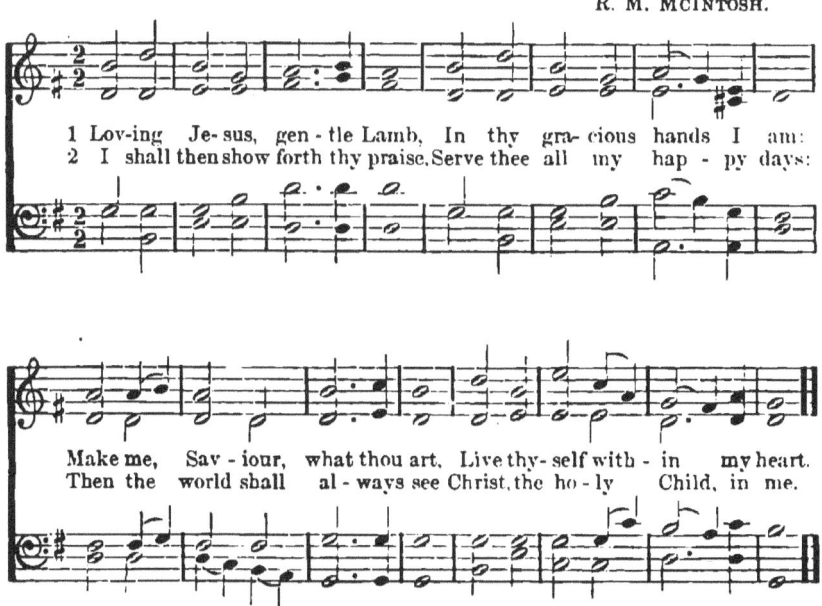

1 Lov-ing Je-sus, gen-tle Lamb, In thy gra-cious hands I am:
2 I shall then show forth thy praise, Serve thee all my hap-py days:
Make me, Sav-iour, what thou art, Live thy-self with-in my heart.
Then the world shall al-ways see Christ, the ho-ly Child, in me.

Copyright, 1886, by R. M. McIntosh.

THE VOICE OF JESUS. Concluded.

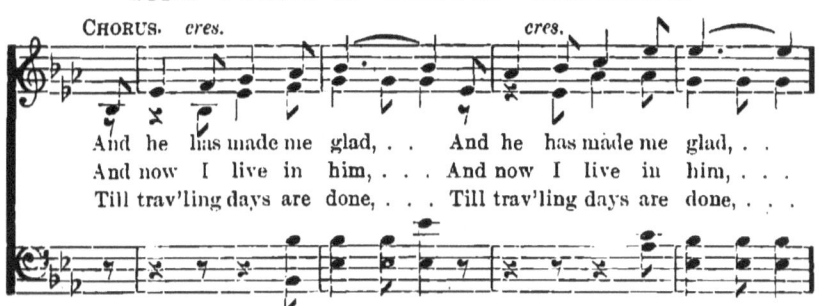

And he has made me glad, . . . And he has made me glad, . . .
And now I live in him, . . . And now I live in him, . . .
Till trav'ling days are done, . . . Till trav'ling days are done, . . .

And he has made me glad, And he has made me glad,
And now I live in him, And now I live in him,
Till trav'ling days are done, Till trav'ling days are done,

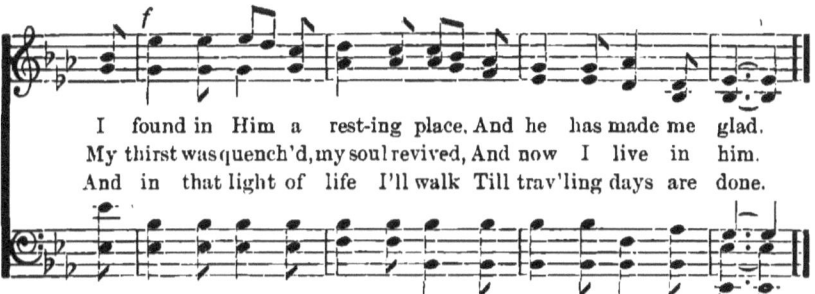

I found in Him a rest-ing place, And he has made me glad.
My thirst was quench'd, my soul revived, And now I live in him.
And in that light of life I'll walk Till trav'ling days are done.

No. 80. HE IS EVER FAITHFUL.

From HAYDN.

1. Let us with a joy-ful mind, Praise the Lord for he is kind;
2. All things liv-ing he doth feed, His full hand sup-plies our need.

All his mer-cies shall en-dure Ev-er faith-ful, ev-er sure.
For his mer-cies shall en-dure, Ev-er faith-ful, ev-er sure.

No. 82. GATHER THE HARVEST.

C. W. Ray. R. M. McIntosh.

1. Gath - er - ing in the har - vest, From val - ley and hill and plain;
2. Gath - er - ing in the har - vest, O'er fields that are rough and wide;
3. Gath - er - ing in the har - vest, With pa-tient and ten- der care;

And gath - er-ing with the reap - ers The rip - en-ing gold- en grain.
And gath - er-ing with the glean-ers A- long by the high-way-side.
The Mas- ter will make us wel- come, The har-vester's joy to share.

REFRAIN.

Per- ish- ing is the har - vest, Precious the sheaves we bring;

Reap-ing for life e - ter - nal, For Je - sus our Sav- iour King.

Copyright, 1892, by R. M. McIntosh.

No. 83. Where The Living Waters Flow.

Words arr.   EDWARD E. NICKERSON by per.

1. Rest to the wea-ry soul And ach-ing breast is giv'n, Down where the
2. For thee, my soul, for thee These priceless joys were bought, Down where the
3. Come, with the ransom'd train, The Saviour's prais-es sing, Down where the
4. And soon, be-fore his face, We'll praise in light a-bove, Down where the

liv-ing waters flow; Grace makes the wounded whole, Love fills our heart with heav'n,
liv-ing waters flow; Thine is the mer-cy free, That Christ to earth has brought,
liv-ing waters flow; Re-joice! the Lamb was slain, Adore! he reigns a king,
liv-ing waters flow; Triumphant thro' his grace, Made perfect by his love,

REFRAIN.

Down where the living waters flow, Down where the living waters flow, living waters flow,

Down where the tree of life doth grow, I'm liv-ing in the light, for

Je-sus and the right, Down where the liv-ing wat-ers flow, living waters flow.

Copyright, 1889, by E. C. Avis, by per.

No. 86. CITY OF THE JASPER WALL.

Dr. BETHUNE. W. A. OGDEN.

1 Oh cit-y of the Jas-per wall, And of the pear-ly gate,
2 Oh cit-y where they need no light Of sun, or moon, or star,
3 Oh cit-y where the shin-ing gates Shut out all grief and sin,

For thee a-mid the storms of life, Our wea-ry spir-its wait,
Could we with eye of faith but see How bright thy mansions are,
Well may we yearn a-mid earth's strife, Thy ho-ly peace to win.—

DUET. p   CHORUS. f

Oh, may we walk the streets of gold, No mor-tal feet have trod;
How soon our doubts would flee a-way, How strong our trust would grow,
Yet will we meek-ly bear the cross, Nor seek to lay it down,

DUET. p   CHORUS. f

Oh, may we wor-ship at the shrine, The tem-ple of our God.
Un-til our hearts should trust no more The treas-ure here be-low.
Un-til our Fa-ther calls us home, And gives the prom-ised crown.

CITY OF THE JASPER WALL. Concluded.

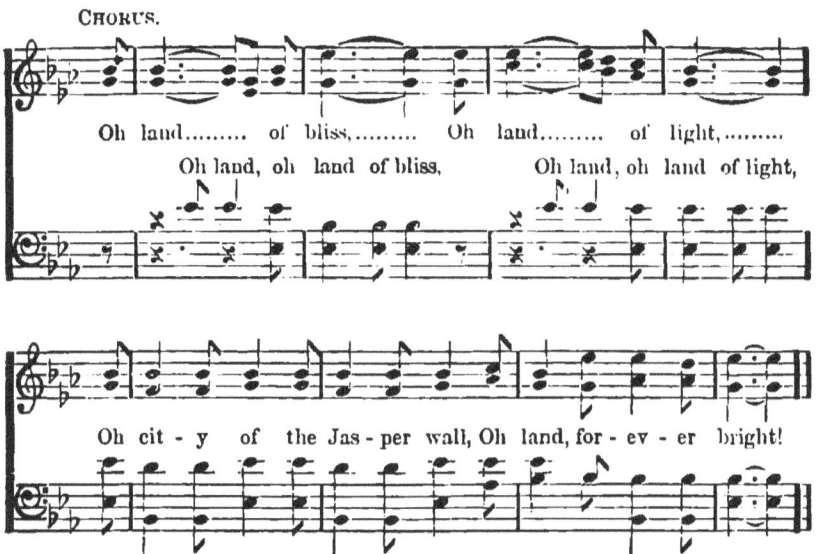

No. 87. CRICHLOW. L. M.

R. M. McIntosh, by per.

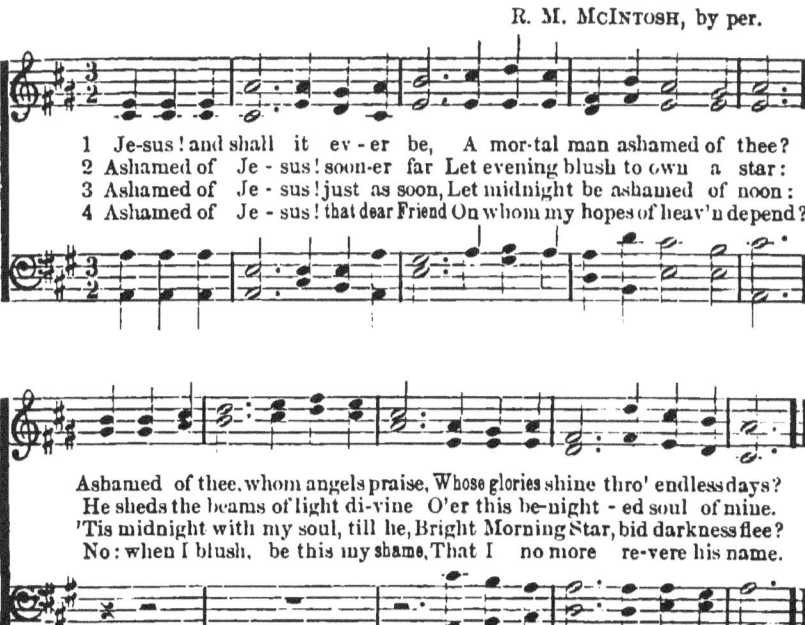

1 Je-sus! and shall it ev-er be, A mor-tal man ashamed of thee?
2 Ashamed of Je-sus! soon-er far Let evening blush to own a star:
3 Ashamed of Je-sus! just as soon, Let midnight be ashamed of noon:
4 Ashamed of Je-sus! that dear Friend On whom my hopes of heav'n depend?

Ashamed of thee, whom angels praise, Whose glories shine thro' endless days?
He sheds the beams of light di-vine O'er this be-night-ed soul of mine.
'Tis midnight with my soul, till he, Bright Morning Star, bid darkness flee?
No: when I blush, be this my shame, That I no more re-vere his name.

No. 88. YON PORTALS FAIR.

ELISHA A. HOFFMAN. R. M. McINTOSH.

1. When shall we stand at yon por- tals fair? By and by, by and by.
2. When will the la - bor of earth be o'er? By and by, by and by.
3. When will we see all our friends a-gain? By and by, by and by.
4. We have a prom- ise of bless- ed rest, By and by, by and by.

When shall we share in the glo - ry there? By and by, yes by and by
When will we sor-row and sigh no more? By and by, yes by and by.
When shall we join them in sweet re-frain? By and by, yes by and by
Lean- ing in calmness on Je - sus' breast, By and by, yes by and by.

'Twill not be long till the Lord shall come, Call me to en- ter my heav'nly home,
Not long on earth can the pilgrim stay; Soon God will summon to heav'n away;
'Twill not be long till in joy we meet, And in af- fec-tion each oth- er greet;
Not here where weary the heart and hand, But in the fair- er Im-manuel's land

There with the ho- ly and blest to roam, Yes, by and by, yes, by and by.
Oh! it is com-ing, that glad, glad day, Yes, by and by, yes, by and by.
Oh! the re - u- nion will be so sweet, Yes, by and by, yes, by and by.
Crown'd with the host of the white-rob'd band, Yes, by and by, yes, by and by.

Copyright, 1892, by R. M. McIntosh.

No. 90. LIVE FOR JESUS.

E. R. Latta. Frank M. Davis.

1. Live for Je - sus, O my brother, His dis - ci - ple ev - er be;
2. Live for Je - sus, wand'ring sinner, Un - der Sa - tan serve no more;
3. Live for Je - sus, O my spir-it, Keep his foot - steps all the way;
4. Live for Je - sus in life's morning; At the noon - tide hour be his,

Ren-der not to a - ny oth - er, What a - lone the Lord's should be.
Of the promised prize a winner Thou may'st be, when life is o'er.
What the Mas - ter bids thee, hear it, And his right-eous will o - bey.
And at eve, when day is turning, And in - her - it endless bliss.

CHORUS.

Live for Je - sus, live for Je - sus; Give him all thou hast to give;

On the cross the world's Redeemer, Gave his life that thou mightst live.

Copyright, 1892, by R. M. McIntosh.

No. 92. WE ARE THY LITTLE LAMBS.

E. A. H.
ELISHA A. HOFFMAN.

1. We are thy lit-tle lambs, Je - sus, dear Sav - iour, Lov - ing and
2. Nev - er for-sake us, Lord; Dai - ly we need thee To guide our
3. Soon on our way we go, Till in yon heav - en, We all thy

serv-ing thee Ev-'ry day; Ev - er be-stow on us Thy lov-ing fav - or.
ten-der feet In the way; Help us be brave and true, Pa-tient and faith-ful,
love shall know, And thy grace, Till at the blessed throne, Gathered to-geth - er,

D.S.—We are thy lit - tle lambs, Thou our Re-deem-er,

FINE.

Help us to walk with thee The nar-row way.
And reach the home a-bove In end - less day. } Our hope is all in thee,
We shall be - hold our Saviour Face to face.
Help us to walk with thee The nar-row way.

D.S.

Thou art our Sav - iour, And from thy counsels we Nev - er would stray:

Copyright, 1892, by R. M. McIntosh.

AT THE FOUNT OF LOVE. Concluded.

Come drink, . . . come free - ly, Come drink . . . to - day;
Come drink,   taste his love

Life's wa - ter free, is of - fer'd thee, Come in the gos - pel way.

No. 95. BROKER.

R. M. McINTOSH, by per.

Softly, gently, yet distinct.

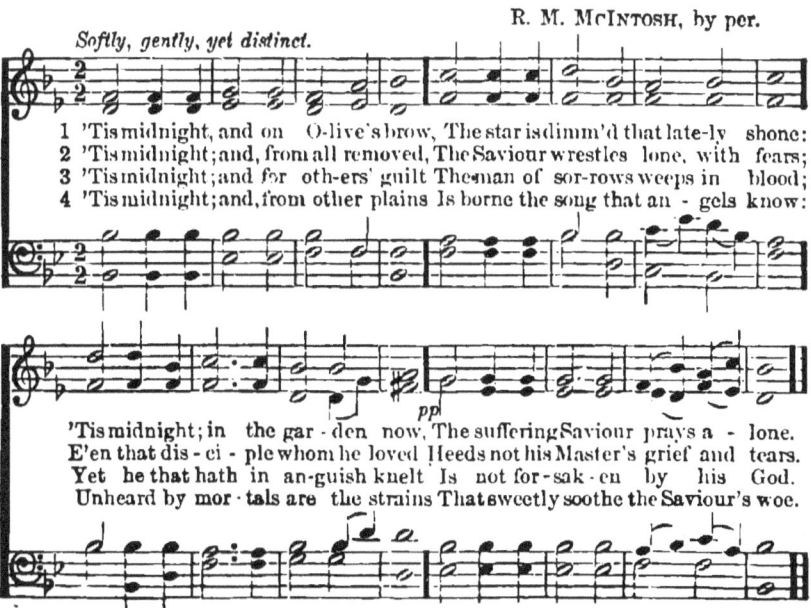

1 'Tis midnight, and on O-live's brow, The star is dimm'd that late-ly shone:
2 'Tis midnight; and, from all removed, The Saviour wrestles lone, with fears;
3 'Tis midnight; and for oth-ers' guilt The man of sor-rows weeps in blood;
4 'Tis midnight; and, from other plains Is borne the song that an - gels know:

'Tis midnight; in the gar - den now, The suffering Saviour prays a - lone.
E'en that dis - ci - ple whom he loved Heeds not his Master's grief and tears.
Yet he that hath in an-guish knelt Is not for-sak - en by his God.
Unheard by mor - tals are the strains That sweetly soothe the Saviour's woe.

No. 98. THE VINEYARD GATE.

Mrs. M. B. C. Slade.　　　　　　　　　　　　　　　R. M. McIntosh.

1. The Master stood at the vineyard gate, And early at morning cried He;
2. So, hour by hour, would He come and see The idlers, and unto them say;
3. The vineyard gate of our Lord Divine, Oh, shall we not en-ter it now?

Oh, laborers, come, nor longer wait, Come work in my vineyard for me.
My vineyard within go al-so ye, Why stand ye here i-dle all day?
He needs us to tend each fruitful vine, His spirit is showing us how.

They toil'd from morn 'till the day was past; The Lord then unto them came,
And then when even was come he bade, His steward all of them call,
And when our la-bor is done, be-low, As fall the shadows of night

And gave to the first, and gave the last, As tho' they had labor'd the same.
And ren-der to each his hire he said, And equal-ly give unto all.
The Lord of us all is just, we know, He'll give us whatever is right.

Copyright, 1892, by R. M. McIntosh.

THE VINEYARD GATE. Concluded.

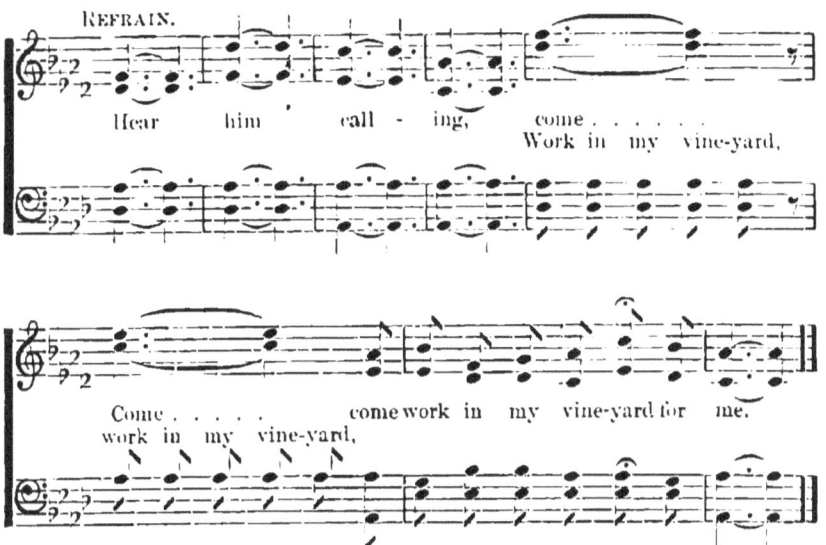

No. 99. PILGRIM.

Fountain E. Pitts. Arr. by R. M. McIntosh.

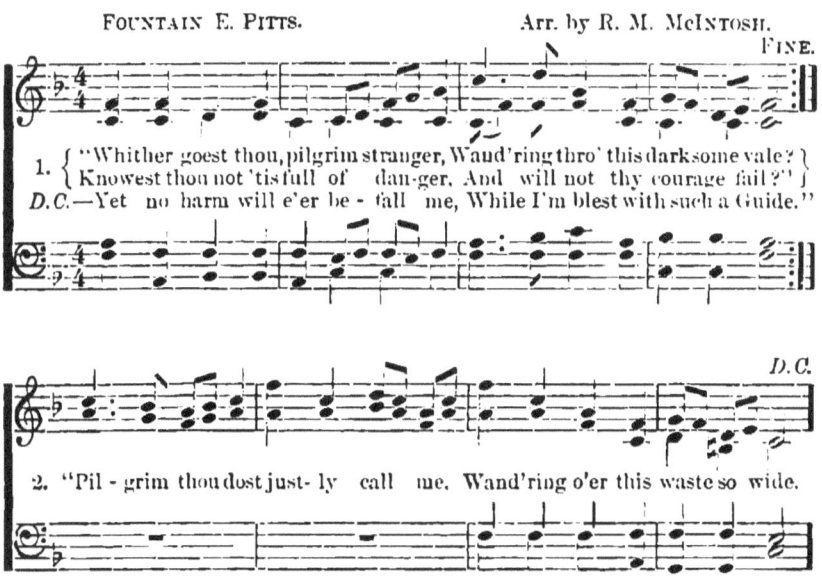

3 "Such a Guide? No guide attends thee—
  Hence, for thee my fears arise:
  If a guardian power befriend thee,
  'Tis unseen by mortal eyes."

4 "Yes, unseen; but still, believe me,
  Such a Guide my steps attends;
  He'll in every strait relieve me,
  He from every harm defends.

LEAVE IT TO HIM. Concluded.

No. 103. LEAVE ME NOT, O GENTLE SAVIOUR.

LIZZIE ASHBAGH.   HARRY J. KURZENKNABE, by per.

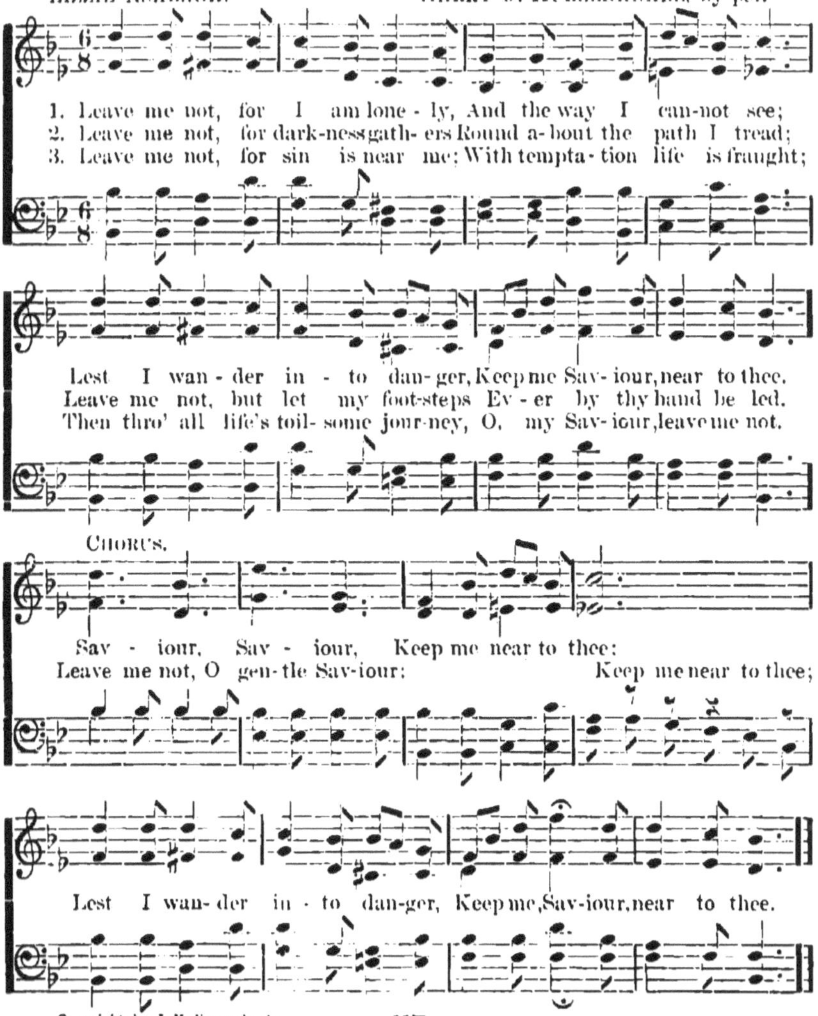

1. Leave me not, for I am lone-ly, And the way I can-not see;
2. Leave me not, for dark-ness gath-ers Round a-bout the path I tread;
3. Leave me not, for sin is near me; With tempta-tion life is fraught;

Lest I wan-der in-to dan-ger, Keep me Sav-iour, near to thee.
Leave me not, but let my foot-steps Ev-er by thy hand be led.
Then thro' all life's toil-some jour-ney, O, my Sav-iour, leave me not.

CHORUS.

Sav-iour, Sav-iour, Keep me near to thee:
Leave me not, O gen-tle Sav-iour; Keep me near to thee;

Lest I wan-der in-to dan-ger, Keep me, Sav-iour, near to thee.

Copyright, by J. H. Kurzenknabe.

No. 106. BRINGING IN THE SHEAVES.

AS DOVES TO THEIR WINDOWS. Concluded.

No. 109. JESUS WILL RECEIVE THEE.

Mrs. HARRIET E. JONES.   FRANK M. DAVIS.

1. Vile and sin - ful, though thou art; Je - sus will re-ceive thee;
2. At the cross there still is room; Je - sus will re-ceive thee;
3. Pre - cious love, so deep and broad; Je - sus will re-ceive thee;

D.C.—Vile and sin - ful, though thou art; Je - sus will re-ceive thee;

On - ly come with con- trite heart, Je - sus will re - ceive thee.
Come and find sweet rest and home, Je - sus will re - ceive thee.
Glo - ry, glo - ry be to God, Je - sus will re - ceive thee.
On - ly come with con- trite heart, Je - sus will re - ceive thee.

Lo the pen - i - ten-tial tear Brings the lov- ing Sav-iour near;
Come with all thy grief and sin, Ask for grace your soul with-in;
Deep - er than the deep- est sin, Last- ing as e - ter - ni - ty,

D. C. for Chorus.

Thy con - fes- sions he will hear; Je - sus will re - ceive thee.
Come, O, come, sweet, heav'n to win; Je - sus will re - ceive thee.
Is our Sav-iour's love to thee Je - sus will re - ceive thee.

Copyright, 1892, by R. M. McIntosh.

IT IS GOOD TO TRUST IN JESUS. Concluded.

THE GOLDEN GATE. Concluded.

No. 112. JESUS, I MY CROSS HAVE TAKEN.

GRANT.   Dr. A. B. EVERETT, by per.

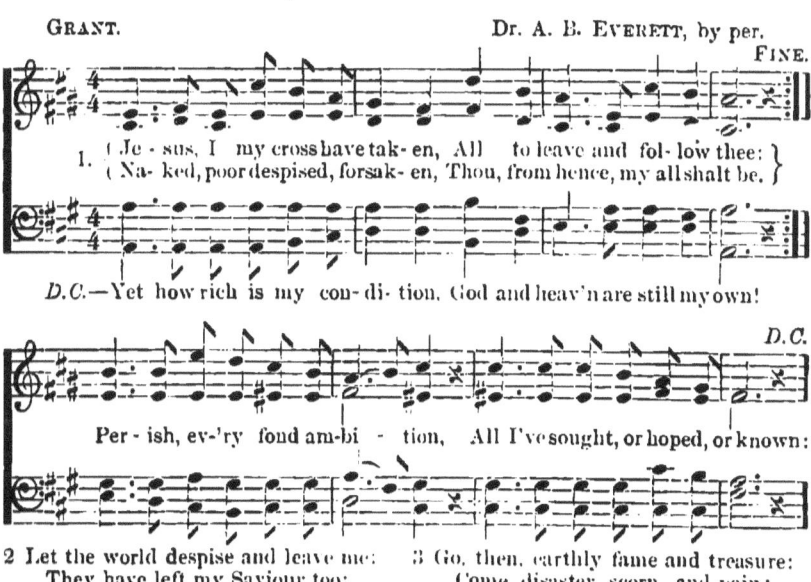

2 Let the world despise and leave me:
They have left my Saviour too:
Human hearts and looks deceive me—
Thou art not, like them untrue.
And while thou shalt smile upon me,
God of wisdom, love, and might,
Foes may hate, and friends disown me,
Show thy face, and all is bright.

3 Go, then, earthly fame and treasure:
Come, disaster, scorn, and pain:
In thy service pain is pleasure—
With thy favor loss is gain.
I have called thee Abba, Father,—
I have set my heart on thee,
Storms may howl, and clouds may gath-
All must work for good to me. [er

IN THE SWEET BY AND BY. Concluded.

by, By and by, We shall rest in the sweet By and by,

sweet By and by.

No. 116. COME UNTO ME, THE SAVIOUR SAID.

LIZZIE ASHBACH.   HARRY J. KURZENKNABE, by per.

1. Come un-to me, the Sav-iour said, And be for-ev - er blest;
2. Take up my yoke, it shall be light, I'll bear a part for thee;
3. For I, the high and ho - ly One, Was meek and low - ly, too;
4. All my com-mands o - bey, and thou Shalt be my hon - ored guest;

Come, all ye wea-ry ones, come near, And I will give you rest.
Come, fol-low in the steps I tread, And meek-ly learn of me.
With rev'rence come and learn of me, My pre - cepts keep in view.
Par - don and peace shall here be thine, And there e - ter - nal rest.

CHORUS.

Come un - to me, ye wea - ry, come, And I will give you rest;

Come, take my yoke and learn of me, And be for-ev - er blest.

Copyright by J. H. Kurzenknabe.

THE WONDERFUL SAVIOUR. Concluded.

In mer-cy for-ev-er and ev-er, Re-mem-ber, remember me.

No. 118. FATHER OF MERCIES.

F. M. D.   DUET AND CHORUS.   FRANK M. DAVIS.

1 Fa-ther of mercies, I come! Come with my burden to thee, Help other than
2 Fa-ther of mercies, I come! Take then this heart 'tis thine own; Refine it and
3 Fa-ther of mercies, I come! Sweetly to rest in thy love; O take me to

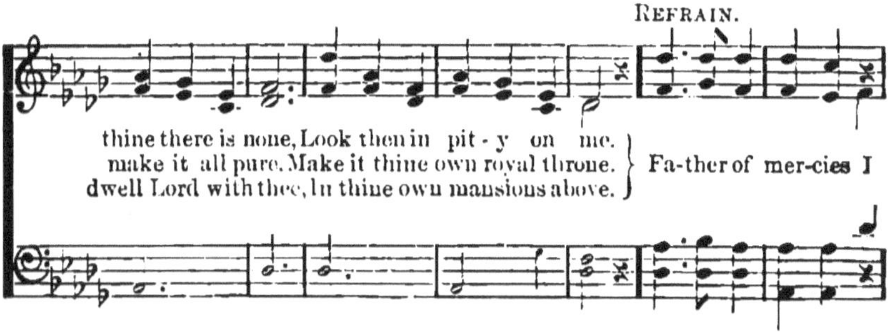

REFRAIN.

thine there is none, Look then in pit-y on me.
make it all pure, Make it thine own royal throne. } Fa-ther of mer-cies I
dwell Lord with thee, In thine own mansions above.

come, I come, Fa-ther of mer-cies I come, I come.

Copyright, 1889, by R. M. McIntosh.

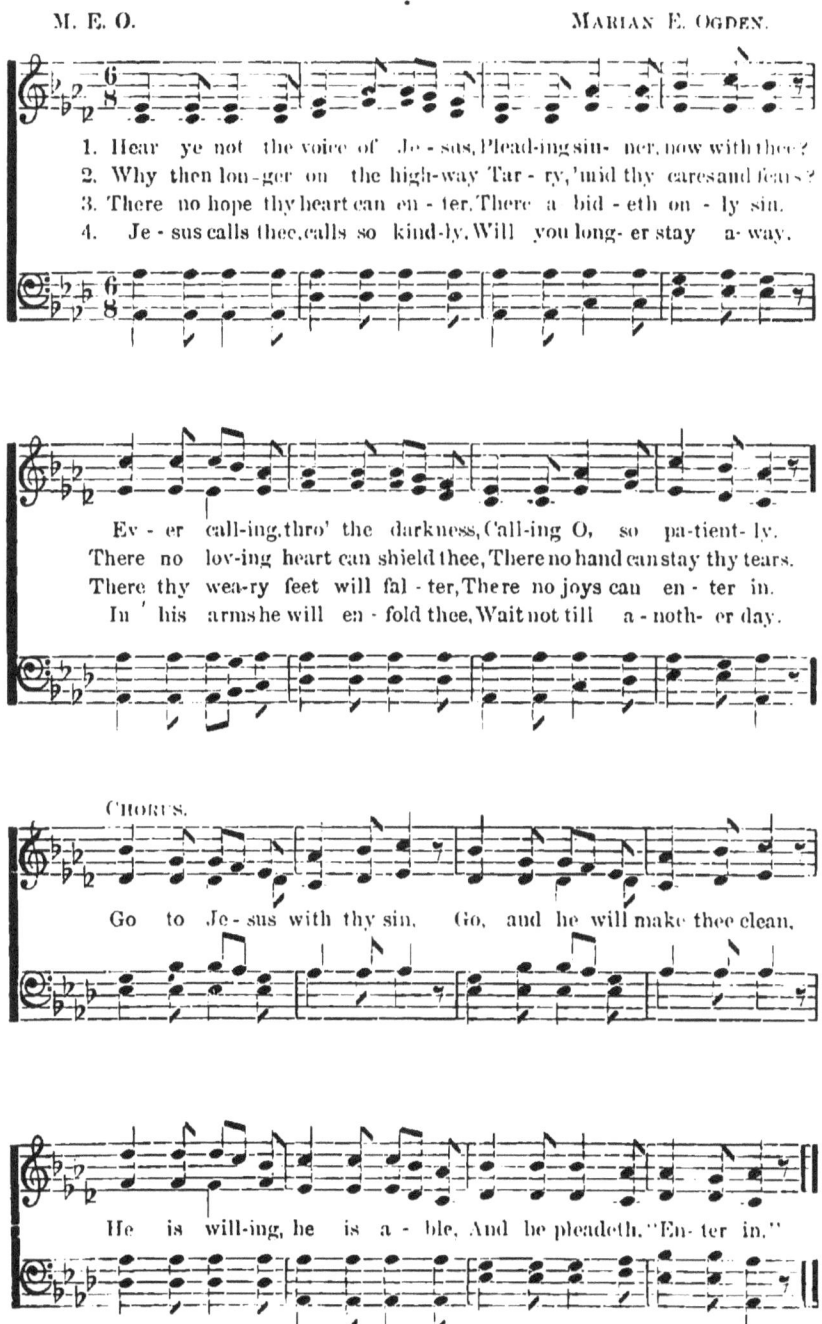

THE SWEETEST SONG. Concluded.

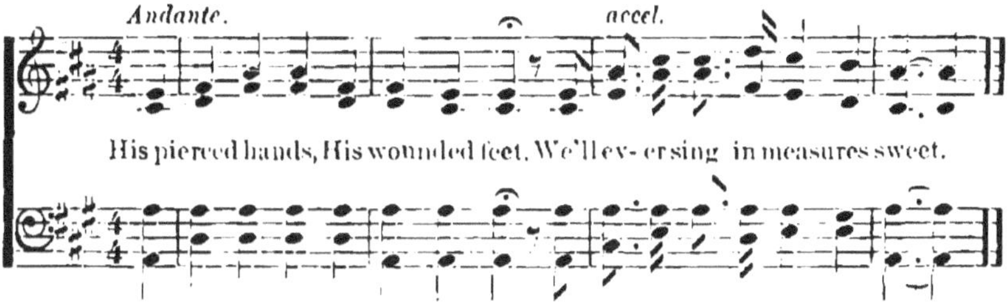
Andante.
accel.
His pierced hands, His wounded feet, We'll ev- er sing in measures sweet.

No. 122. JESUS WILL LET YOU IN.

A. S K. A. S. KIEFFER, by per.

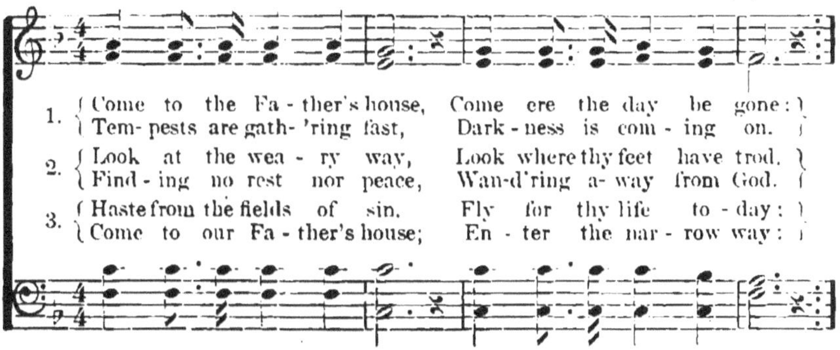
1. { Come to the Fa - ther's house, Come ere the day be gone: }
{ Tem- pests are gath- 'ring fast, Dark - ness is com - ing on. }
2. { Look at the wea - ry way, Look where thy feet have trod, }
{ Find - ing no rest nor peace, Wan-d'ring a- way from God. }
3. { Haste from the fields of sin, Fly for thy life to - day: }
{ Come to our Fa - ther's house; En - ter the nar - row way: }

CHORUS.

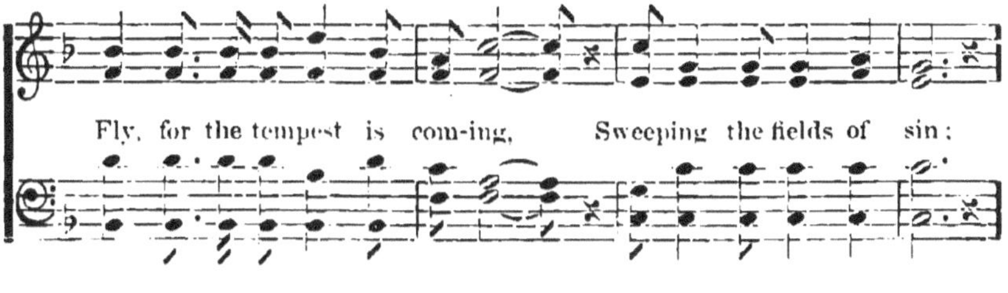
Fly, for the tempest is com-ing, Sweeping the fields of sin:

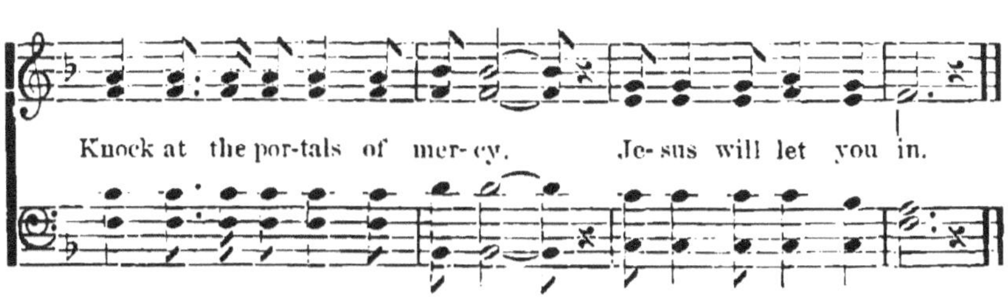
Knock at the por-tals of mer- cy, Je- sus will let you in.

No. 123. THERE IS A LAND IMMORTAL.

THOMAS MACKELLAR.   R. M. MCINTOSH.

1. There is a land im-mor-tal, The beau-ti-ful of lands;
2. That glo-rious land is Heav-en, And Death the sen-try grim
3. Tho' dark and drear the pas-sage That lead-eth to the gate,
4. Their sighs are lost in sing-ing; They're bless-ed in their tears;

Be-side its an-cient por-tal A sen-try grim-ly stands.
The Lord there-of has giv-en The open-ing keys to him;
Yet grace at-tends the mes-sage To souls that watch and wait;
Their jour-ney heav'n ward winging, They leave on earth their fears.

He on-ly can un-do it, And o-pen wide the door;
And ran-som'd spir-its, sigh-ing And sor-row-ful for sin,
And at the time ap-point-ed A mes-sen-ger comes down,
Death like an an-gel seem-ing, "We wel-come thee!" they cry:

And mor-tals who pass thro' it Are mor-tals nev-er-more;
Pass thro' the gate in dy-ing, And free-ly en-ter in,
And guides the Lord's a-noint-ed From cross to glo-ry's crown
Their face with glo-ry gleam-ing, 'Tis life for them to die,

Copyright, 1892, by R. M. McIntosh.

THERE IS A LAND IMMORTAL. Concluded.

No. 124. LEBANON. 7s

Dr. A. B. EVERETT, by per.

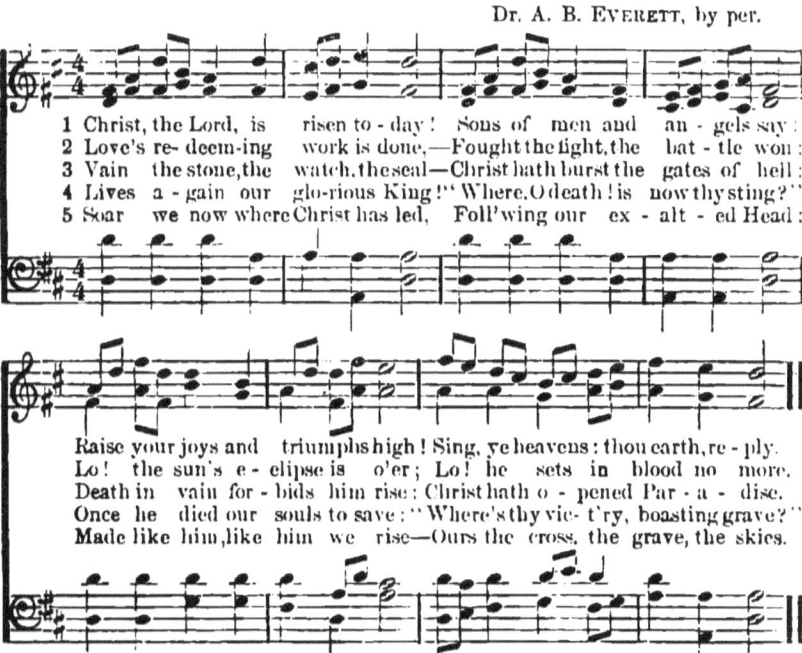

I Lean on His Wonderful Might. Concluded.

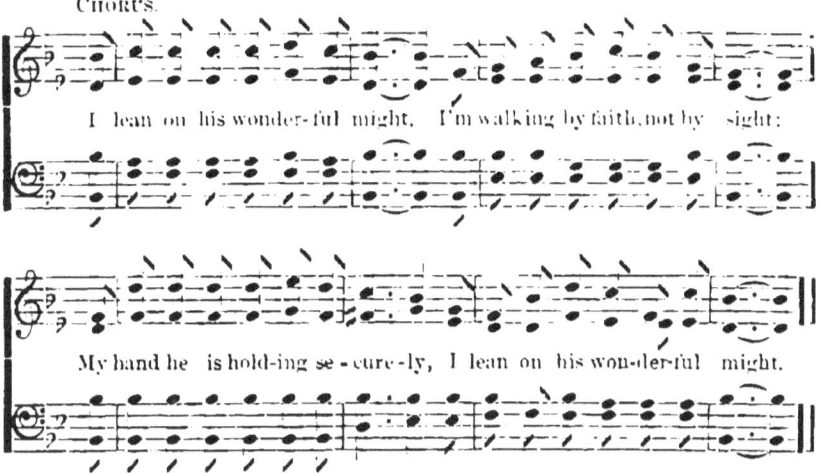

No. 126. COME TO JESUS JUST NOW.

1. Come to Jesus, come to Jesus, Come to Jesus just now; Just now come to Jesus, Come to Jesus just now.
2. He will save you, he will save you, He will save you just now; Just now he will save you, He will save you just now.
3. Don't reject him, don't reject him, Don't reject him just now; Just now don't reject him, Don't reject him just now.

4 He is ready, he is ready,
   He is ready just now;
   Just now he is ready, &c.

5 Oh, believe him, oh, believe him,
   Oh, believe him just now;
   Just now oh, believe him, &c.

6 Do not tarry, do not tarry,
   Do not tarry just now;
   Just now do not tarry, &c.

7 Hallelujah, hallelujah,
   Hallelujah, Amen;
   Amen, hallelujah, &c.

No. 127. RAISE ALOFT THE STANDARD.

LAURA E. NEWELL.   FRANK M. DAVIS.

1. Raise a-loft the stand-ard, Let the col-ors fly; See our loy-al ar-my Proud-ly mov-ing by: Je-sus, is the Cap-tain, Of our might-y band, Sound the song of tri-umph, O-ver sea and land.
2. Raise a-loft the stand-ard, Be its folds unfurled; Tell to ev-'ry peo-ple, God doth rule the world; Her-ald his sal-va-tion, Now from shore to shore, Till each land and na-tion, Shall our God a-dore.
3. Raise a-loft the ban-ner, In the ranks stand fast; Soldiers true and val-iant, Fight un-til the last; Bat-tle brave and loy-al, Ev-er as you go, Till you reach his pas-ture, Where still waters flow.

CHORUS.

Glo-ry in the high-est, Je-sus leads the way; Glo-ry in the high-est, Com-eth no dis-may; Raise a-loft the stan-dard,

Copyright, 1892, by Gospel Advocate Pub. Co.

RAISE ALOFT THE STANDARD. Concluded.

Let the col-ors fly, Je-sus is our Lead-er; On to vic-to-ry!

No. 128.   ZERAH.   C. M.

JOHN MORRISON.   LOWELL MASON.

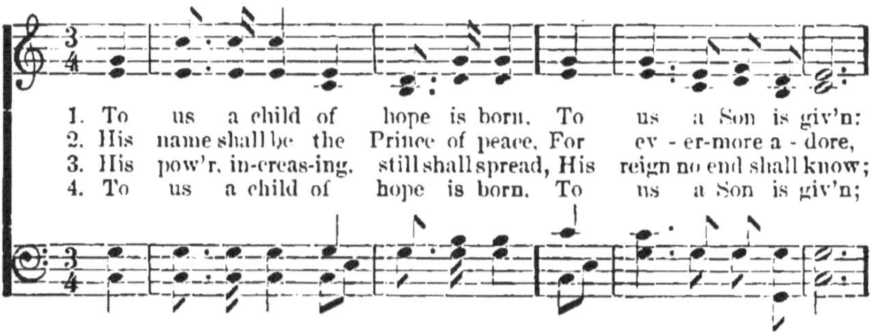

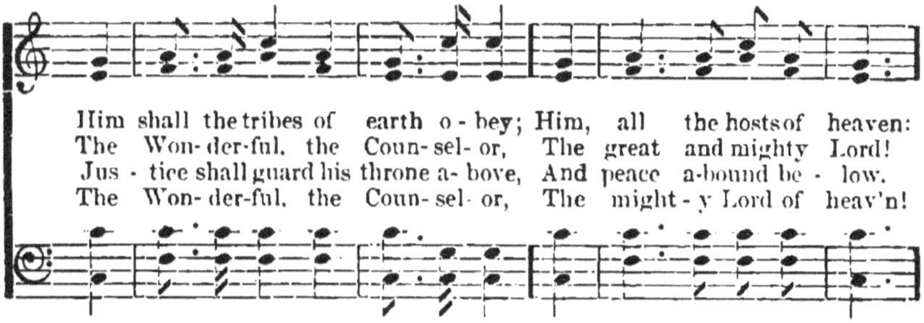

1. To us a child of hope is born, To us a Son is giv'n:
2. His name shall be the Prince of peace, For ev-er-more a-dore,
3. His pow'r, in-creas-ing, still shall spread, His reign no end shall know;
4. To us a child of hope is born, To us a Son is giv'n;

Him shall the tribes of earth o-bey; Him, all the hosts of heaven:
The Won-der-ful, the Coun-sel-or, The great and mighty Lord!
Jus-tice shall guard his throne a-bove, And peace a-bound be-low.
The Won-der-ful, the Coun-sel-or, The might-y Lord of heav'n!

Him shall the tribes of earth o-bey; Him, all the hosts of heav'n.
The Wonder-ful, the Counsel-or, The great and might-y Lord!
Justice shall guard his throne a-bove, And peace a-bound be-low.
The Wonder-ful, the Coun-sel-or, The mighty Lord of heav'n!

IT WILL NEVER GROW OLD. Concluded

al-ways be day; It glad-dens my heart with a joy that's un-told,
To think of that land that will nev-er grow old.

No. 130. MANOAH. C. M.

S. STENNETT. GREATOREX.

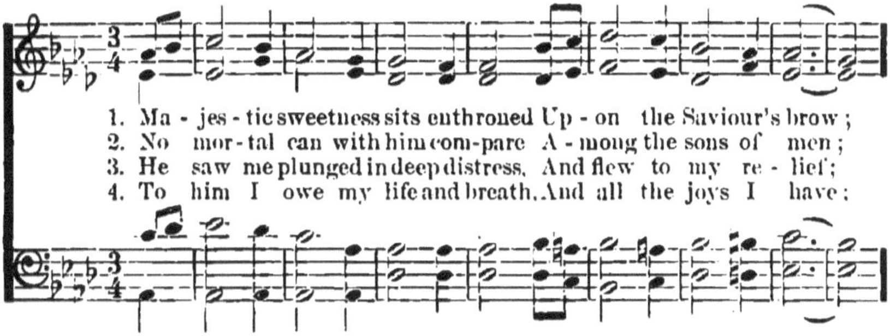

1. Ma - jes - tic sweetness sits enthroned Up - on the Saviour's brow;
2. No mor - tal can with him com-pare A - mong the sons of men;
3. He saw me plunged in deep distress, And flew to my re - lief;
4. To him I owe my life and breath, And all the joys I have;

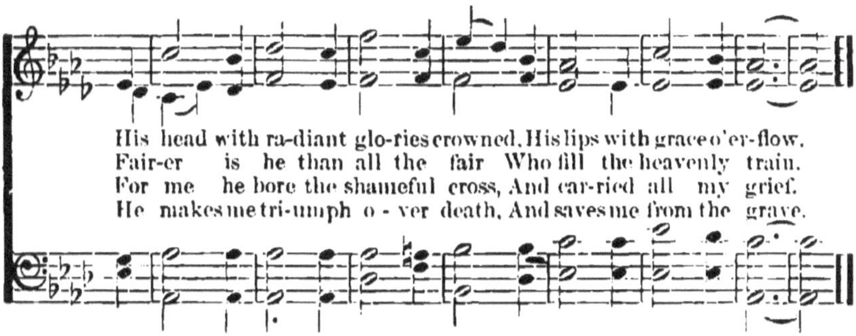

His head with ra-diant glo-ries crowned, His lips with grace o'er-flow.
Fair-er is he than all the fair Who fill the heavenly train.
For me he bore the shameful cross, And car-ried all my grief.
He makes me tri-umph o - ver death, And saves me from the grave.

5 To heaven, the place of his abode,
He brings my weary feet;
Shows me the glories of my God,
And makes my joys complete.

6 Since from thy bounty I receive
Such proofs of love divine,
Had I a thousand hearts to give,
Lord, they should all be thine.

WE SHALL MEET AGAIN. Concluded.

No. 132. AZMON. C. M.

ISAAC WATTS.

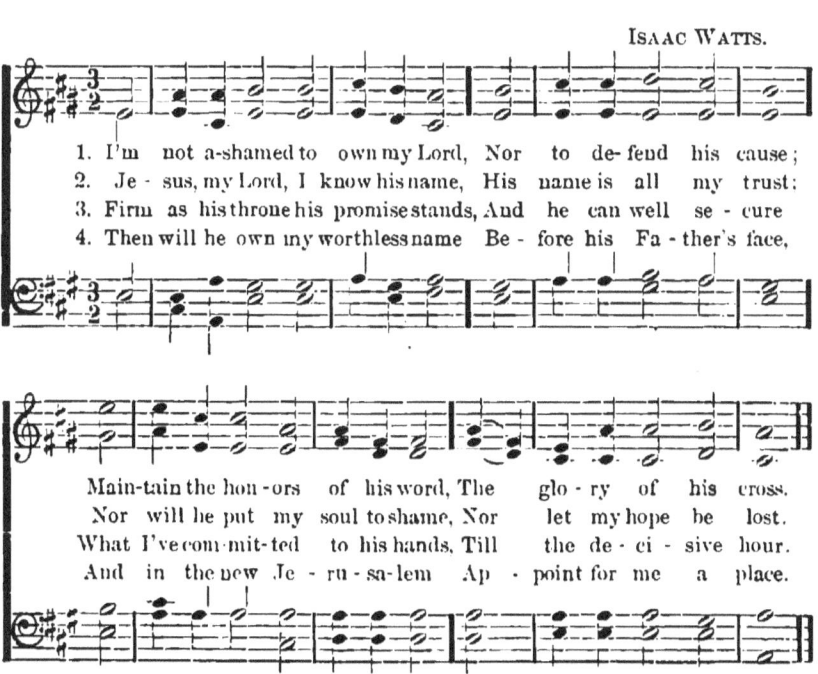

No. 133. The Lessons are all about Jesus our Lord.

JULIA H. JOHNSTON.   FRANK M. DAVIS.

1. The lessons are all about Jesus, our Lord, The Saviour who came from above; Of his wonderful birth, and his life on the earth; Of his goodness and mercy and love.
2. The lessons are all about Jesus, our Lord, The little one's Saviour and friend; For he calls us to come to his heavenly home; He will love us, and keep to the end.
3. The lessons are all about Jesus, our Lord, O beautiful story of old; Let us hear and obey till the shepherd shall say, "Enter into my heavenly fold."

CHORUS.

The lessons are all about, Jesus our Lord; The life, and the truth, and the way; All the poor and distressed, he both

Copyright, 1892, by R. M. McIntosh.

The Lessons are all about Jesus. Concluded.

pit - ied and bless'd, As he taught them and help'd them each day.

No. 134. BETHANY.

Mrs. S. F. Adams.   Lowell Mason, by per.

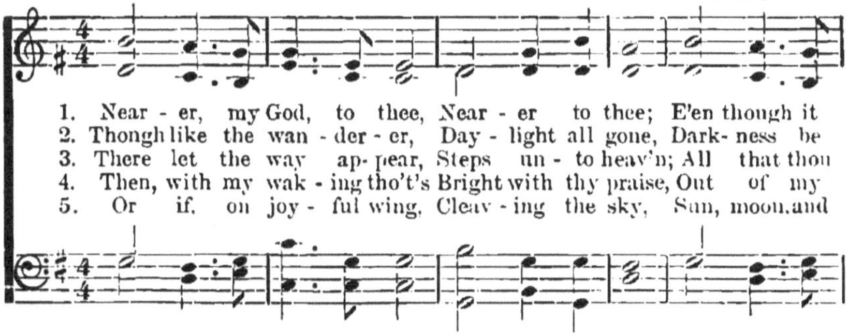

1. Near - er, my God, to thee, Near - er to thee; E'en though it
2. Though like the wan - der - er, Day - light all gone, Dark- ness be
3. There let the way ap- pear, Steps un - to heav'n; All that thou
4. Then, with my wak - ing tho't's Bright with thy praise, Out of my
5. Or if, on joy - ful wing, Cleav - ing the sky, Sun, moon, and

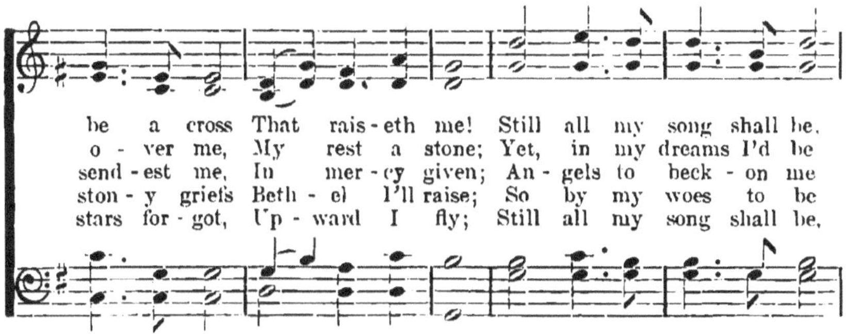

be a cross That rais - eth me! Still all my song shall be,
o - ver me, My rest a stone; Yet, in my dreams I'd be
send - est me, In mer - cy given; An - gels to beck - on me
ston - y griefs Beth - el I'll raise; So by my woes to be
stars for - got, Up - ward I fly; Still all my song shall be,

Near- er, my God, to thee! Near- er, my God, to thee, Near-er to thee!

O Think of His Wonderful Love. Concluded.

all of his good-ness to thee; 'Twas he that redeemed thee and

made thee whole, And set thee e - ter - nal - ly free.

No. 138. ASHVILLE. C. M.

Dr. A. B. Everett, by per.

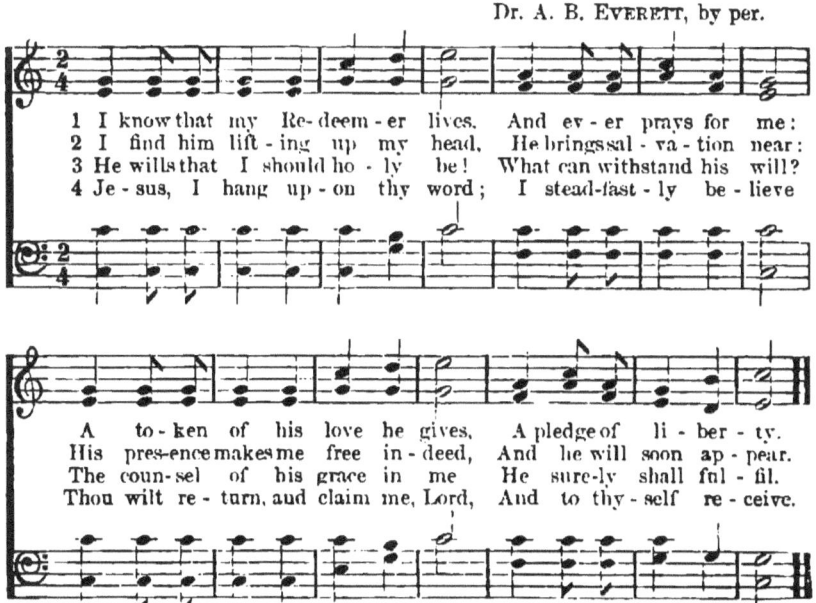

1 I know that my Re-deem-er lives, And ev-er prays for me:
2 I find him lift-ing up my head, He brings sal - va - tion near:
3 He wills that I should ho - ly be! What can withstand his will?
4 Je - sus, I hang up - on thy word; I stead-fast - ly be - lieve

A to-ken of his love he gives, A pledge of li - ber - ty.
His pres-ence makes me free in - deed, And he will soon ap - pear.
The coun-sel of his grace in me He sure-ly shall ful - fil.
Thou wilt re - turn, and claim me, Lord, And to thy-self re - ceive.

PLEADING WITH THEE. Concluded.

No. 140. KAVANAUGH. L. M.

R. M. McIntosh, by per.

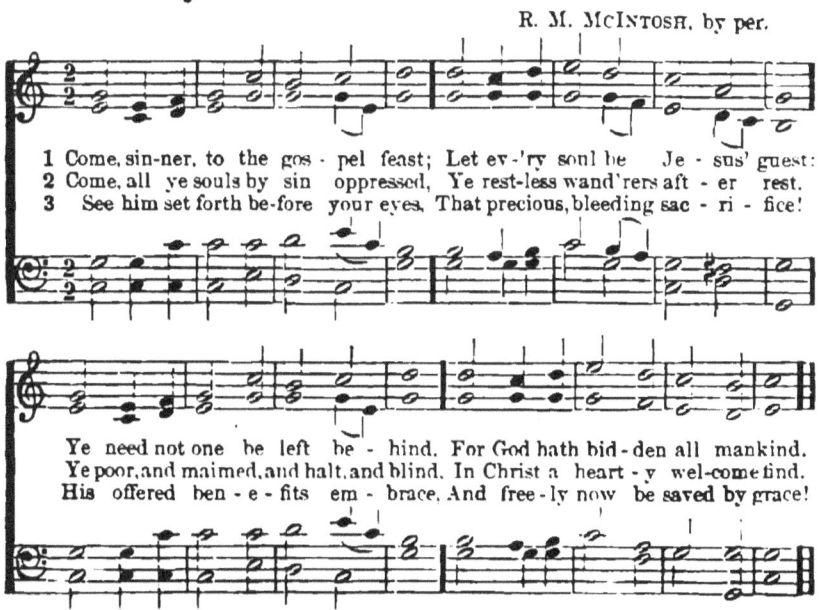

1 Come, sin-ner, to the gos - pel feast; Let ev-'ry soul be Je - sus' guest:
2 Come, all ye souls by sin oppressed, Ye rest-less wand'rers aft - er rest.
3 See him set forth be-fore your eyes, That precious, bleeding sac - ri - fice!

Ye need not one be left be - hind, For God hath bid - den all mankind.
Ye poor, and maimed, and halt, and blind, In Christ a heart - y wel-come find.
His offered ben - e - fits em - brace, And free - ly now be saved by grace!

STEADILY MARCHING ON. Concluded.

CHURCH RALLYING SONG. Concluded.

No. 144. THE SAVIOUR IS MY ALL IN ALL.

P. B. P. BILHORN.

1. The Saviour is my all in all, He is my constant theme!
2. His promise gives sweet peace within, And bids all care depart?
3. And whatsoever I may ask, To glorify his name,
4. Oh, praise the Lord, my soul, rejoice, Give thanks unto thy God!

By fully trusting in his word He keeps me pure and clean.
He fills my soul with righteousness, And purifies the heart.
The Father freely gives to me, Since Christ the Saviour came.
Who took thee in thy sinfulness, And cleansed thee by his blood!

CHORUS.

Glory! oh, glory! Jesus hath redeemed me;
Glory! oh, glory! He washed my sins away, away!

Copyright, 1888, by P. Bilhorn.

No. 145. SEEK FOR THE WANDERERS.

C. W. R.
C. W. Ray.

1. Ye friends of the bless-ed Re-deem-er, Go seek for the wand-'rers a-stray; Thro' des-erts or lanes of the cit-y, Wher-ev-er they wan-der a-way. Some soul may be wea-ry and lan-guish-ing, Be-wildered and suf-fer-ing there; Some soul may be
2. O has-ten to those who in sor-row, May per-ish with hun-ger and cold, O haste and wait not for the mor-row, Go bring to the shel-ter-ing fold. O haste to the mountains so bleak and bare, A-midst the dark by-ways of sin: Go seek them with
3. Go quick-ly the mo-ments are fly-ing, The fee-ble and fal-ter-ing bring; They soon may be starv-ing and dy-ing, Bring in to the feast of the King. A man-sion a-bove with the glo-ri-fied, By Je-sus the King shall be giv'n; A seat with his

Copyright, 1892, by C. W. Ray.

Arise, Shine; for thy Light is come. Continued.

No. 147. WHAT A FRIEND WE HAVE.

C. C. CONVERSE, by per.

1. What a Friend we have in Je - sus, All our sins and griefs to bear;
2. Have we tri- als and tempta- tions? Is there trou-ble a - ny-where?
3. Are we weak and heavy la - den, Cumbered with a load of care?

What a priv - i - lege to car - ry Ev - 'ry thing to God in prayer.
We should nev-er be dis- cour- aged, Take it to the Lord in prayer.
Pre-cious Sav-iour, still our ref - uge,—Take it to the Lord in prayer.

O, what peace we oft - en for - feit, O, what needless pain we bear,
Can we find a friend so faith - ful, Who will all our sor-rows share?
Do thy friends despise, for- sake thee? Take it to the Lord in prayer;

All be-cause we do not car - ry Ev - 'ry thing to God in prayer.
Je - sus knows our ev - 'ry weak-ness: Take it to the Lord in prayer.
In his arms he'll take and shield thee, Thou wilt find a sol- ace there.

No. 148. OLD HUNDRED. L. M.

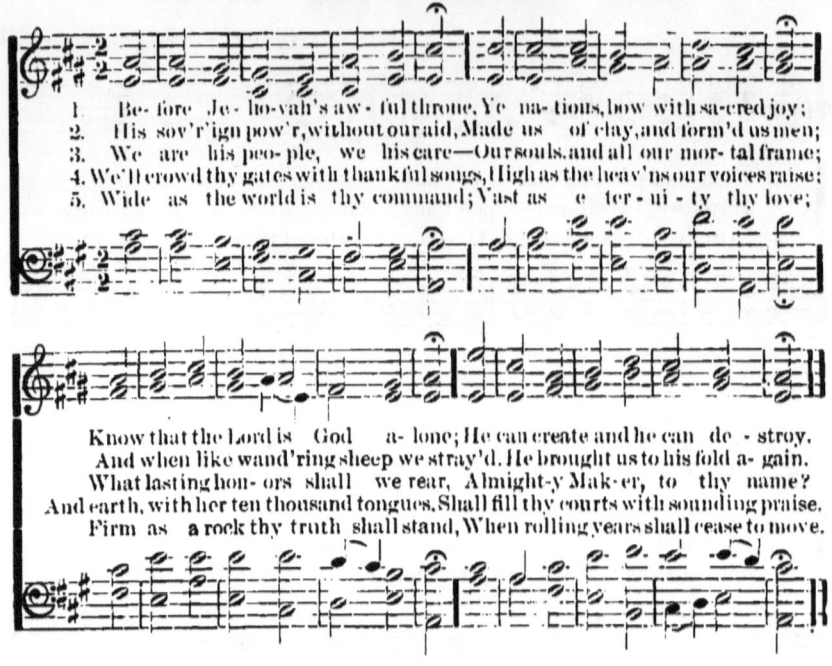

1. Be-fore Je-ho-vah's aw-ful throne, Ye na-tions, bow with sa-cred joy;
2. His sov'r'ign pow'r, without our aid, Made us of clay, and form'd us men;
3. We are his peo-ple, we his care—Our souls, and all our mor-tal frame;
4. We'll crowd thy gates with thankful songs, High as the heav'ns our voices raise;
5. Wide as the world is thy command; Vast as e-ter-ni-ty thy love;

Know that the Lord is God a-lone; He can create and he can de-stroy.
And when like wand'ring sheep we stray'd, He brought us to his fold a-gain.
What lasting hon-ors shall we rear, Almight-y Mak-er, to thy name?
And earth, with her ten thousand tongues, Shall fill thy courts with sounding praise.
Firm as a rock thy truth shall stand, When rolling years shall cease to move.

No. 149. TRURO. L. M.

CHARLES BURNEY.

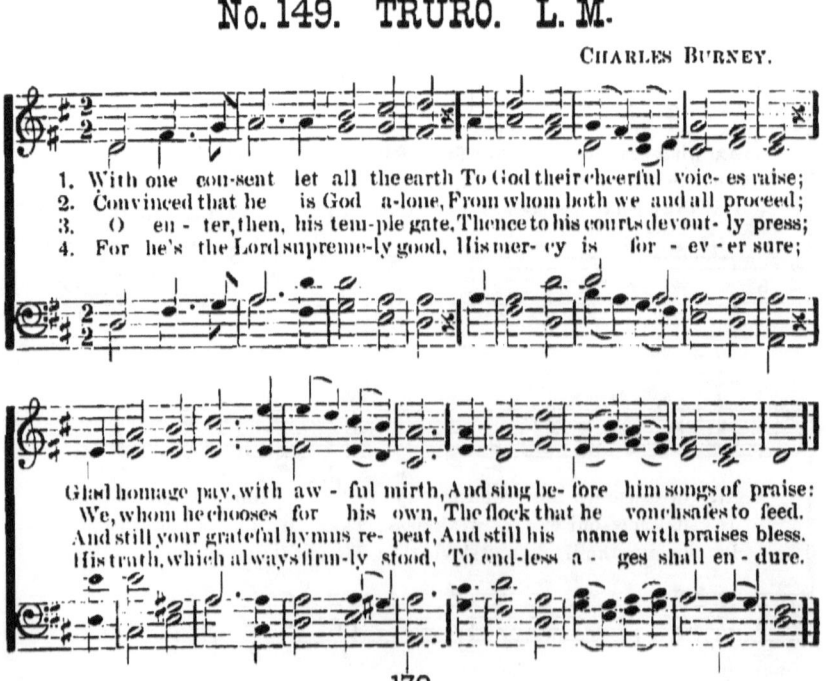

1. With one con-sent let all the earth To God their cheerful voic-es raise;
2. Convinced that he is God a-lone, From whom both we and all proceed;
3. O en-ter, then, his tem-ple gate, Thence to his courts devout-ly press;
4. For he's the Lord supreme-ly good, His mer-cy is for-ev-er sure;

Glad homage pay, with aw-ful mirth, And sing be-fore him songs of praise.
We, whom he chooses for his own, The flock that he vouchsafes to feed.
And still your grateful hymns re-peat, And still his name with praises bless.
His truth, which always firm-ly stood, To end-less a-ges shall en-dure.

No. 152. REST. L. M.

WM. B. BRADBURY.

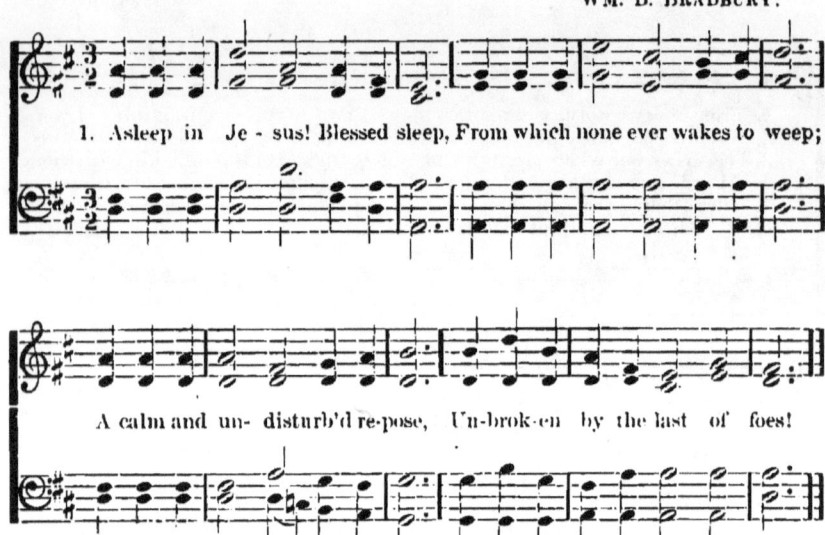

1. Asleep in Jesus! Blessed sleep, From which none ever wakes to weep;
A calm and un-disturb'd re-pose, Un-brok-en by the last of foes!

2 Asleep in Jesus! O how sweet
To be for such a slumber meet;
With holy confidence to sing,
That death has lost its venomed sting!

3 Asleep in Jesus! Peaceful rest,
Whose waking is supremely blest!
No fear, no woe, shall dim the hour
That manifests the Saviour's power.

4 Asleep in Jesus! O for me
May such a blissful refuge be!
Securely shall my ashes lie,
And wait the summons from on high.

5 Asleep in Jesus! Time nor space
Affects this precious hiding-place;
On Indian plains, on Lapland snows,
Believers find the same repose.

6 Asleep in Jesus! Far from thee
Thy kindred and their graves may be;
But thine is still a blessed sleep,
From which none ever wakes to weep.

No. 153. L. M.

1 I know that my Redeemer lives—
What comfort this sweet sentence gives;
He lives, he lives, who once was dead!
He lives, my ever-living Head.

2 He lives, to bless me with his love;
He lives, to plead for me above;
He lives, my hungry soul to feed;
He lives, to bless in time of need:

3 He lives, to grant me rich supply;
He lives, to guide me with his eye;
He lives, to comfort me when faint;
He lives, to hear my soul's complaint.

4 He lives, my kind, wise, heavenly Friend;
He lives, and loves me to the end;
He lives, and while he lives I'll sing,
He lives, my Prophet, Priest, and King;

5 He lives, all glory to his name;
He lives, my Saviour, still the same—
O the sweet joy this sentence gives:
I know that my Redeemer lives.

No. 154. L. M.

1 Come weary souls, with sin distress'd;
The Saviour offers heavenly rest;
The kind, the gracious call obey,
And cast your gloomy fears away.

2 Oppressed with guilt, a heavy load,
O come, and bow before your God.
Divine compassion, mighty love,
Will all the painful load remove.

3 Here mercy's boundless ocean flows,
To cleanse your guilt and heal your woes;
Pardon, and life, and endless peace—
How rich the gift, how free the grace!

No. 155. ARLINGTON. C. M.

1. How sweet, how heav'nly is the sight, When those that love the Lord
2. When each can feel his brother's sigh, And with him bear a part;
3. When, free from en-vy, scorn, and pride, Our wishes all a-bove,
4. When love in one de-light-ful stream, Thro' ev-'ry bo-som flows;
5. Love is the gold-en chain that binds The hap-py souls a-bove;

In one an-oth-er's peace delight, And so ful-fill the word;
When sor-row flows from eye to eye, And joy from heart to heart;
Each can his brother's fail-ings hide, And show a brother's love;
When un-ion sweet and dear esteem In ev-'ry ac-tion glows!
And he's an heir of heav'n who finds His bo-som glow with love.

No. 156. REMEMBER ME.

R. BURNHAM. Anon.

1. Je-sus, thou art the sinner's friend; As such I look to thee;
REF.—Re-mem-ber me, re-mem-ber me, O Lord, re-mem-ber me.

Now, in the full-ness of thy love, O Lord, re-mem-ber me.
Now, in the full-ness of thy love, O Lord, re-mem-ber me.

2 Remember thy pure word of grace,
  Remember Calvary;
Remember all thy promises,
  And then remember me.—REF.
3 I own I'm guilty, own I'm vile;
  Yet thy salvation's free;

Then in thy all-abounding grace,
  O Lord, remember me.—REF.
4 And when I close my eyes in death,
  And creature helps all flee,
Then, O my great Redeemer, Lord,
  I pray, remember me.—REF.

No. 157. HOME. C. M.

ELIZABETH MILLS. R. M. McINTOSH, by per.

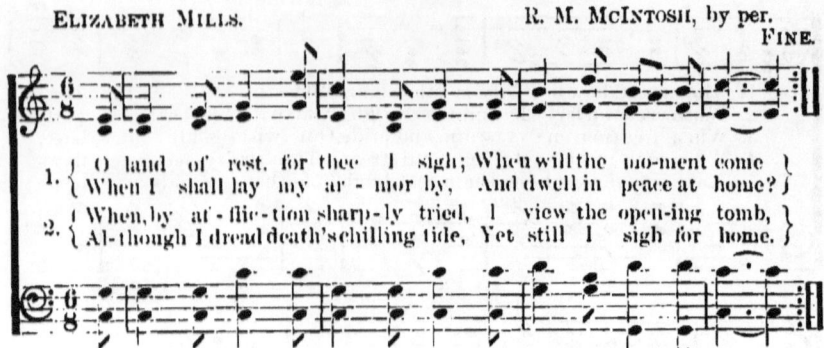

1. { O land of rest, for thee I sigh; When will the mo-ment come
   { When I shall lay my ar-mor by, And dwell in peace at home? }
2. { When, by af-flic-tion sharp-ly tried, I view the open-ing tomb,
   { Al-though I dread death's chilling tide, Yet still I sigh for home. }

D. C.—This world's a wil-der-ness of woe, This world is not my home.
I long to quit th' unhallowed ground, And dwell with Christ at home.

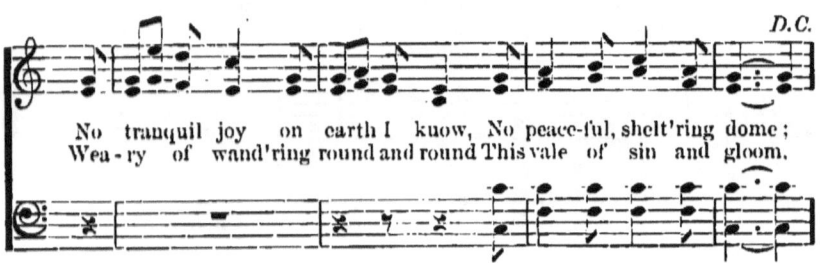

No tranquil joy on earth I know, No peace-ful, shelt'ring dome;
Wea-ry of wand'ring round and round This vale of sin and gloom.

No. 158. C. M.

1 Jesus, I love thy charming name;
   'Tis music to my ear;
   Fain would I sound it out so loud
   That all the earth might hear.

2 Yes, thou art precious to my soul,
   My transport and my trust;
   Jewels to thee are gaudy toys,
   And gold is sordid dust.

3 All that my ardent soul can wish,
   In thee doth richly meet;
   Nor to my eyes is light so dear,
   Nor friendship half so sweet.

4 Thy grace shall dwell upon my heart,
   And shed its fragrance there—
   The noblest balm of all its wounds,
   The cordial of its care.

No. 159. C. M.

1 Happy the home, when God is there,
   And love fills every breast;
   Where one their wish, and one their prayer,
   And one their heavenly rest.

2 Happy the home, where Jesus' name
   Is sweet to every ear;
   Where children early lisp his fame,
   And parents hold him dear.

3 Happy the home where prayer is heard,
   And praise is wont to rise;
   Where parents love the sacred word,
   And live but for the skies.

4 Lord, let us in our homes agree
   This blessed peace to gain;
   Unite our hearts in love to thee,
   And love to all will reign.

No. 160. C. M.

1 Hosanna to our conquering King!
   All hail, incarnate Love!
   Ten thousand songs and glories wait
   To crown thy head above.

2 Thy victories and thy deathless fame
   Through all the world shall run,
   And everlasting ages sing
   The triumphs thou hast won.

No. 161. DUKE STREET. L. M.

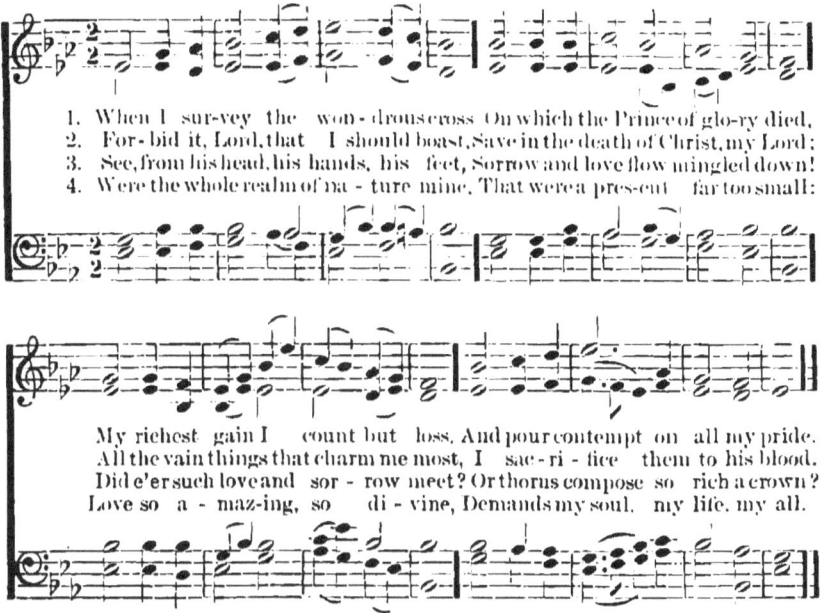

1. When I survey the wondrous cross On which the Prince of glory died,
2. Forbid it, Lord, that I should boast, Save in the death of Christ, my Lord;
3. See, from his head, his hands, his feet, Sorrow and love flow mingled down!
4. Were the whole realm of nature mine, That were a present far too small;

My richest gain I count but loss, And pour contempt on all my pride.
All the vain things that charm me most, I sacrifice them to his blood.
Did e'er such love and sorrow meet? Or thorns compose so rich a crown?
Love so amazing, so divine, Demands my soul, my life, my all.

No. 162. HEBRON. L. M.

Dr. L. Mason.

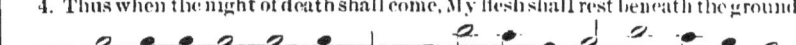

1. Thus far the Lord hath led me on, Thus far his pow'r prolongs my days,
2. Much of my time has run to waste, And I perhaps am near my home;
3. I lay my body down to sleep, Peace is the pillow for my head;
4. Thus when the night of death shall come, My flesh shall rest beneath the ground.

And ev'ry evening shall make known Some fresh memorial of his grace.
But he forgives my follies past, And gives me strength for days to come.
While well-appointed angels keep Their watchful stations round my bed.
And wait thy voice to rend my tomb, With sweet salvation in the sound.

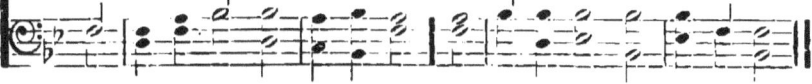

No. 163. SUMMERS. L. M.

R. M. McIntosh, by per.

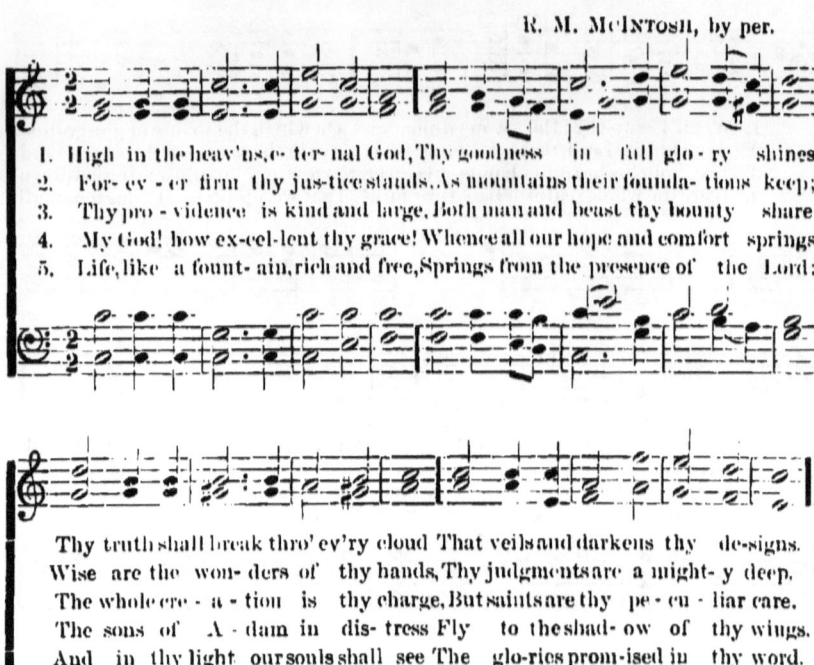

1. High in the heav'ns, e-ter-nal God, Thy goodness in full glo-ry shines;
2. For-ev-er firm thy jus-tice stands, As mountains their founda-tions keep;
3. Thy pro-vidence is kind and large, Both man and beast thy bounty share;
4. My God! how ex-cel-lent thy grace! Whence all our hope and comfort springs:
5. Life, like a fount-ain, rich and free, Springs from the presence of the Lord;

Thy truth shall break thro' ev'ry cloud That veils and darkens thy de-signs.
Wise are the won-ders of thy hands, Thy judgments are a might-y deep.
The whole cre-a-tion is thy charge, But saints are thy pe-cu-liar care.
The sons of A-dam in dis-tress Fly to the shad-ow of thy wings.
And in thy light our souls shall see The glo-ries prom-ised in thy word.

No. 164. L. M.

1 Jehovah reigns; he dwells in light,
Arrayed with majesty and might;
The world, created by his hands,
Still on its firm foundation stands.

2 But ere this spacious world was made,
Or had its first foundation laid,
His throne eternal ages stood,
Himself the Ever-living God.

3 Forever shall his throne endure;
His promise stands forever sure;
And everlasting holiness
Becomes the dwellings of his grace.

No. 165. L. M.

1 King Jesus, reign forevermore,
Unrivaled in thy courts above,
While we, with all thy saints, adore
The wonders of redeeming love.

2 No other Lord but thee we'll know,
No other power but thine confess;
We'll spread thine honors while below,
And heaven shall hear us shout thy grace.

3 We'll sing along the heavenly road
That leads us to thy blest abode;
Till, with the vast, unnumbered throng,
We join in heaven's triumphant song:

4 Till, with pure hands and voices sweet,
We cast our crowns at Jesus' feet,
And sing of everlasting love,
In everlasting strains above.

No. 166. L. M.

1 From all that dwell below the skies,
Let the Creator's praise arise;
Let the Redeemer's name be sung
Through every land, by every tongue.

2 Eternal are thy mercies, Lord;
Eternal truth attends thy word;
Thy praise shall sound from shore to shore
Till suns shall rise and set no more.

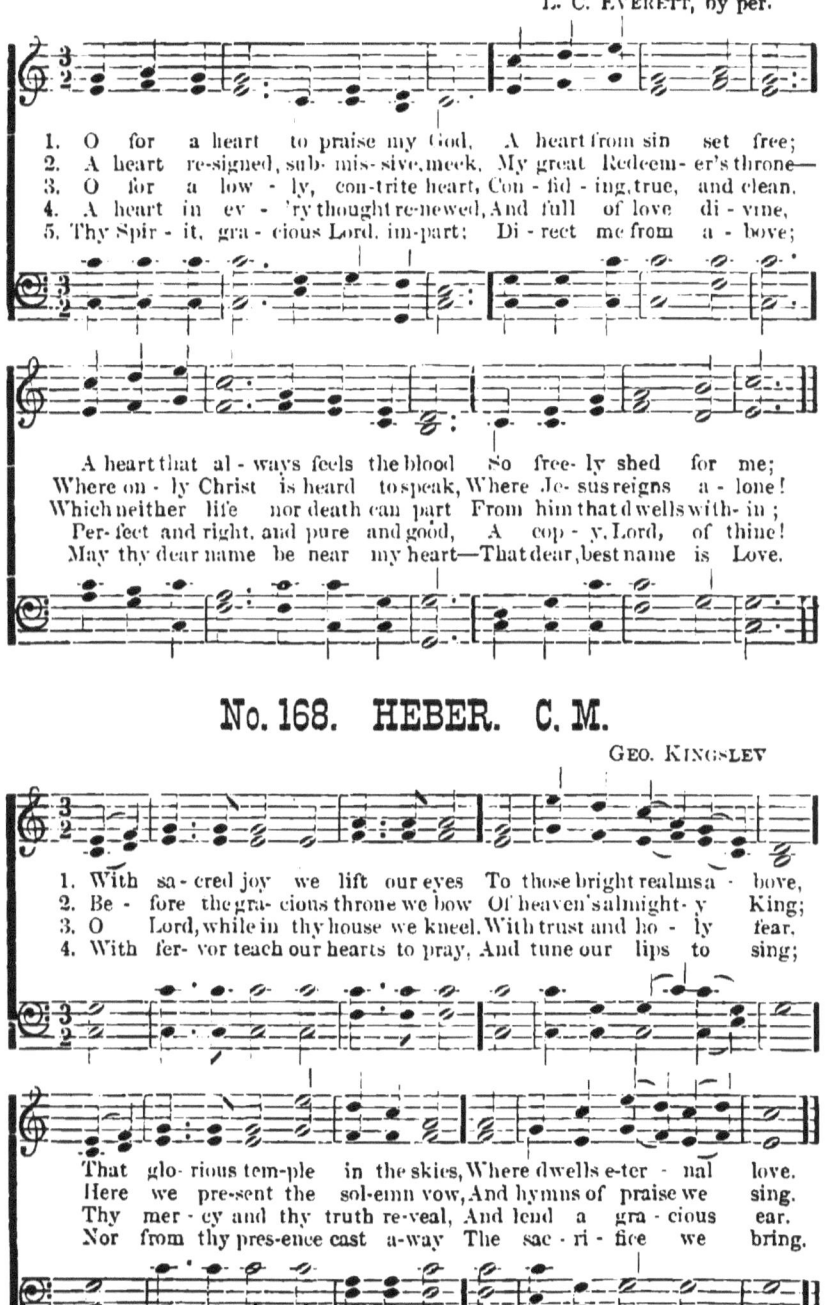

No. 169. DOGGETT. C. M.

R. M. McIntosh, by per.

1. Since I can read my title clear To mansions in the skies, I bid farewell to every fear, And wipe my weeping eyes.

2 Should earth against my soul engage,
  And fiery darts be hurled,
 Then I would smile at Satan's rage,
  And face a frowning world.

3 Let cares, like a wild deluge, come,
  And storms of sorrow fall,

May I but safely reach my home,
 My God, my heaven, my all.

4 There shall I bathe my weary soul
  In seas of heavenly rest;
 And not a wave of trouble roll
  Across my peaceful breast.

No. 170. ORTONVILLE. C. M.

Dr. Hastings.

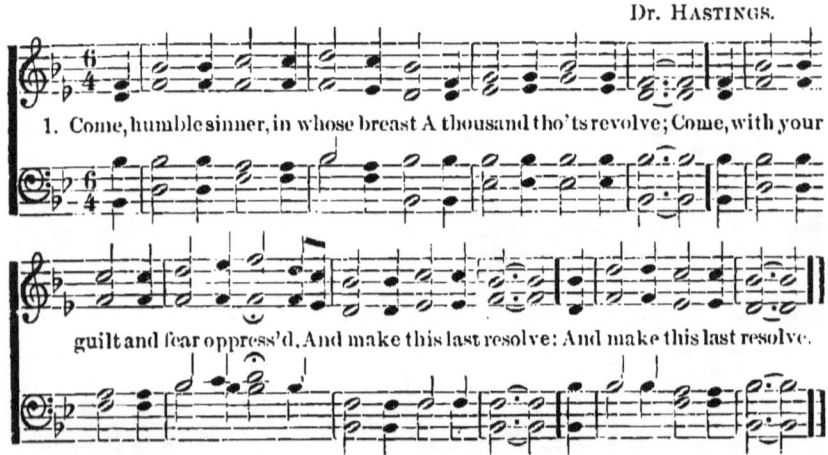

1. Come, humble sinner, in whose breast A thousand tho'ts revolve; Come, with your guilt and fear oppress'd, And make this last resolve: And make this last resolve.

2 I'll go to Jesus, though my sin
  Has like a mountain rose;
 His kingdom now I'll enter in,
  Whatever may oppose.

3 Humbly I'll bow at his command,
  And there my guilt confess;
 I'll own I am a wretch undone,
  Without his sovereign grace.

4 Surely he will accept my plea,
  For he has bid me come;
 Forthwith I'll rise, and to him flee,
  For yet, he says, there's room.

5 I can not perish if I go:
  I am resolved to try:
 For if I stay away, I know
  I must forever die.

No. 171. NAOMI. C. M.

H. G. NAGELI.

1. Father, whate'er of earthly bliss Thy sovereign will denies,
Accepted at thy throne of grace, Let this petition rise.

2 Give me a calm, a thankful heart,
From every murmur free;
The blessings of thy grace impart,
And make me live to thee;

3 Let the sweet hope that thou art mine
My life and death attend;
Thy presence through my journey shine,
And crown my journey's end.

No. 172. C. M.

1 In memory of the Saviour's love
We keep the sacred feast,
Where every humble, contrite heart
Is made a welcome guest.

2 Under his banner thus we sing
The wonders of his love,
And thus anticipate by faith
The heavenly feast above.

No. 173. SILOAM. C. M.

I. B. WOODBURY.

1. Think gently of the erring one; O let us not forget,
However darkly stain'd by sin, He is our brother yet:

2 Heir of the same inheritance,
Child of the self-same God,
He hath but stumbled in the path
We have in weakness trod.

3 Speak gently to the erring ones:
We yet may lead them back,

With holy words and tones of love,
From misery's thorny track.

4 Forget not, brother, thou hast sinned,
And sinful yet may be;
Deal gently with the erring heart,
As God hath dealt with thee.

No. 174. HARP. C. M.

Arr. by R. M. McIntosh.

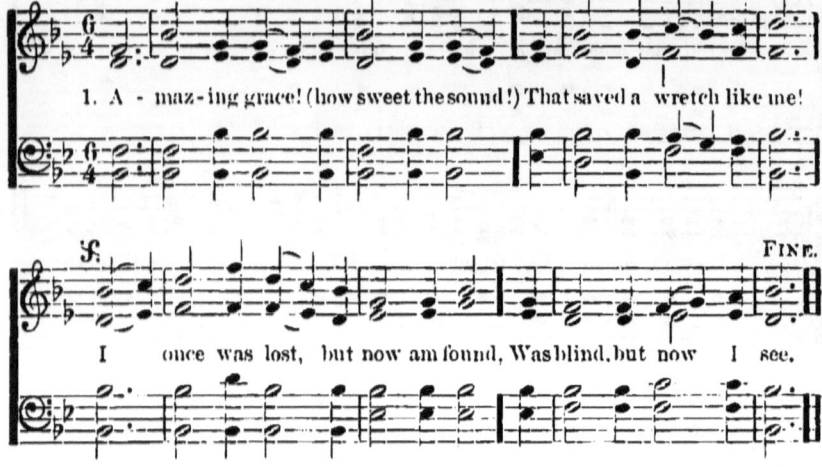

By per. R. M. McIntosh.

2 'Twas grace that taught my heart to fear,
  And grace my fears relieved ;
  How precious did that grace appear,
  The hour I first believed !

3 Thro' many dangers, toils, and snares,
  I have already come ;
  'Tis grace has brought me safe thus far,
  And grace will lead me home.

4 The Lord has promised good to me ;
  His word my hope secures :
  He will my shield and portion be
  As long as life endures.

5 Yea, when this flesh and heart shall fail,
  And mortal life shall cease,
  I shall possess, within the veil,
  A life of joy and peace.

No. 175. C. M.

1 What shall I render to my God
  For all his kindness shown?
  My feet shall visit thine abode,
  My songs address thy throne.

2 Among the saints who fill thy house,
  My offering shall be paid;
  There shall my zeal perform the vows
  My soul, in anguish, made.

3 How happy all thy servants are !
  How great thy grace to me !
  My life, which thou hast made thy care,
  Lord, I devote to thee.

4 Now I am thine, forever thine;
  Nor shall my purpose move;
  Thy hand hath loosed my bonds of pain,
  And bound me with thy love.

5 Here, in thy courts, I leave my vow,
  And thy rich grace record;
  Witness, ye saints, who hear me now,
  If I forsake the Lord.

No. 176. CHRISTMAS. C. M.

HANDEL.

1. Awake, my soul, stretch ev'ry nerve, And press with vigor on; A heav'n-ly race demands thy zeal, And an immortal crown, And an immortal crown.

2 A cloud of witnesses around
Hold thee in full survey;
Forget the steps already trod,
And onward urge thy way.

3 'Tis God's all-animating voice
That calls thee from on high;
'Tis his own hand presents the prize,
To thine aspiring eye.

4 Blest Saviour, introduced by thee,
Have I my race begun;
And, crowned with victory, at thy feet
I'll lay my honors down.

No. 177. C. M.

1 Rise, O my soul, pursue the path
By ancient heroes trod;
Ambitious view those holy men
Who lived and walked with God.

2 Though dead, they speak in reason's ear,
And in example live;
Their faith and hope and mighty deeds
Still fresh instruction give.

3 'Twas through the Lamb's most precious blood
They conquered every foe;
And to his power and matchless grace
Their crowns and honor owe.

4 Lord, may we ever keep in view
The patterns thou hast given,
And ne'er forsake the blesséd road
Which led them safe to heaven.

No. 178. C. M.

1 Come, let us join, with one accord,
In hymns around the throne;
This is the day our risen Lord
Hath made and called his own.

2 This is the day which God hath blest,
The brightest of the seven,
Type of the everlasting rest
The saints enjoy in heaven.

3 Then let us in his name sing on,
And hasten on that day
When our Redeemer shall come down,
And shadows pass away.

No. 179. BALERMA. C. M.

R. SIMPSON.

1. O thou who driest the mourner's tear, How dark this world would be, If when deceiv'd and wounded here, We could not fly to thee.

2 But thou wilt heal the broken heart
 Which, like the plants that throw
 Their fragrance from the wounded part,
 Breathes sweetness out of woe.

3 When joy no longer soothes or cheers,
 And e'en the hope that threw

A moment's sparkle o'er our tears
 Is dimmed and vanished too—

4 Then sorrow, touched by thee, grows bright
 With more than rapture's ray;
 The darkness shows us worlds of light
 We never saw by day.

No. 180. MEAR. C. M.

AARON WILLIAMS.

1. O God of Beth-el, by whose hand Thy peo-ple still are fed, Who thro' this wea-ry pil-grim-age Hast all our fa-thers led!

2 Our vows, our prayers we now present
 Before thy throne of grace:
 God of our fathers, be the God
 Of their succeeding race.

3 Through each succeeding path of life
 Our wandering footsteps guide;
 Give us each day our daily bread,
 And raiment fit provide.

4 O spread thy covering wings around,
 Till all our wanderings cease,
 And at our Father's loved abode
 We all arrive in peace.

5 Such blessing from thy gracious hand
 Our humble prayers implore;
 And thou shalt be our chosen God,
 Our portion evermore.

No. 181. WOODLAND. C. M.

N. D. GOULD.

1. With joy we med-i-tate the grace Of our High Priest a-bove; His heart is full of ten-der-ness, His heart is full of ten-der-ness, His bos-om glows with love.

2 Touched with a sympathy within,
  He knows our feeble frame;
  He knows what sore temptations mean,
  For he has felt the same.

3 He, in the days of feeble flesh,
  Poured out his cries and tears;
  And in his measure feels afresh
  What every member bears.

4 Then let our humble faith address
  His mercy and his power;
  We shall obtain delivering grace
  In each distressing hour.

No. 182. C. M.

1 What glory gilds the sacred page,
  Majestic, like the sun!
  It gives a light to every age;
  It gives, but borrows none.

2 The hand that gave it still supplies
  His gracious light and heat;
  His truths upon the nations rise;
  They rise, but never set.

3 Let everlasting thanks be thine,
  For such a bright display,
  As makes the world of darkness shine
  With beams of heavenly day.

4 My soul rejoices to pursue
  The paths of truth and love,
  Till glory breaks upon my view
  In brighter worlds above.

No. 183. C. M.

1 How precious is the book divine,
  By inspiration given!
  Bright as a lamp its precepts shine,
  To guide our souls to heaven.

2 It sweetly cheers our drooping hearts
  In this dark vale of tears:
  Life, light, and joy, it still imparts,
  And quells our rising fears.

3 This lamp, through all the tedious night
  Of life, shall guide our way,
  Till we behold the clearer light
  Of an eternal day.

No. 184. AVON. C. M.

HUGH WILSON.

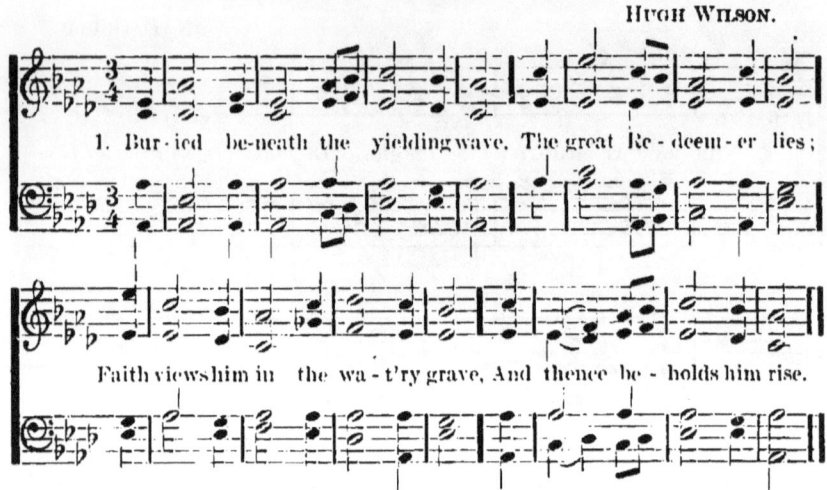

1. Buried beneath the yielding wave, The great Redeemer lies; Faith views him in the wa-t'ry grave, And thence beholds him rise.

2 And thus do willing souls, to-day,
  Their ardent zeal express,
And, in the Lord's appointed way,
  Fulfill all righteousness.

3 With joy we in his footsteps tread,
  And would his cause maintain;
Like him be numbered with the dead,
  And with him rise and reign.

4 Now we, blest Saviour, would to thee
  Our grateful voices raise;
Washed in the fountain of thy blood,
  Our lives shall be thy praise.

No. 185. VAUGHAN. C. M.

R. M. McINTOSH, by per.

1. When languor and disease invade This trembling house of clay, 'Tis sweet to look beyond my pains, And long to fly away;

2 Sweet to look inward, and attend
  The whispers of his love;
Sweet to look upward to the place
  Where Jesus pleads above;

3 Sweet to look back and see my name
  In life's fair book set down;

Sweet to look forward, and behold
  Eternal joys my own;

4 Sweet to rejoice in lively hope
  That when my chance shall come,
Angels shall hover round my bed,
  And waft my spirit home.

No. 186. SOLITUDE. C. M.

L. C. EVERETT, by per.

1. There is a name I love to hear, I love to speak its worth;

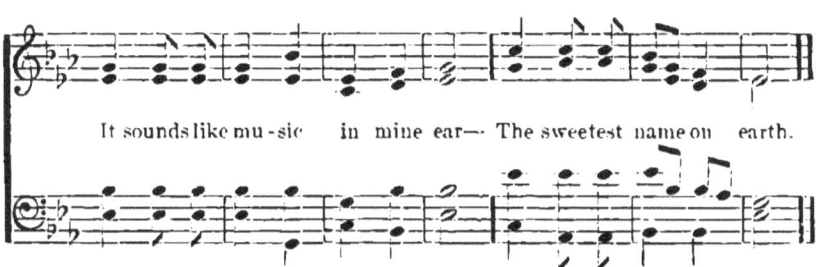

It sounds like mu-sic in mine ear— The sweetest name on earth.

2 It tells me of a Saviour's love,
Who died to set me free:
It tells me of his precious blood,
The sinner's perfect plea.

3 Jesus! the name I love so well,
The name I love to hear!
No saint on earth its worth can tell,
No heart conceive how dear.

4 This name shall shed its fragrance still
Along this thorny road:
Shall sweetly smooth the rugged hill
That leads me up to God.

No. 187. C. M.

1 Thou art the Way: to thee alone
From sin and death we flee;
And he who would the Father seek,
Must seek him, Lord, by thee.

2 Thou art the Truth: thy word alone
True wisdom can impart:
Thou, only, canst inform the mind,
And purify the heart.

3 Thou art the Life: the rending tomb
Proclaims thy conquering arm:
And those who put their trust in thee,
Nor death nor hell shall harm.

4 Thou art the Way, the Truth, the Life:
Grant us that way to know,
That truth to keep, that life to win,
Whose joys eternal flow.

No. 188. C. M.

1 Jesus, in thy transporting name,
What blissful glories rise—
Jesus, the angels' sweetest theme,
The wonder of the skies!

2 Well might the skies with wonder view
A love so strange as thine:
No thought of angels ever knew
Compassion so divine.

3 Jesus, and didst thou leave the sky
To bear our sins and woes?
And didst thou bleed and groan and die,
For vile, rebellious foes?

4 Victorious love! can language tell
The wonders of thy power,
Which conquered all the force of hell
In that tremendous hour!

5 What glad return can I impart
For favors so divine?
O take this heart, this worthless heart,
And make it only thine!

No. 189. DUNDEE. C. M.

GUILLAUME FRANC.

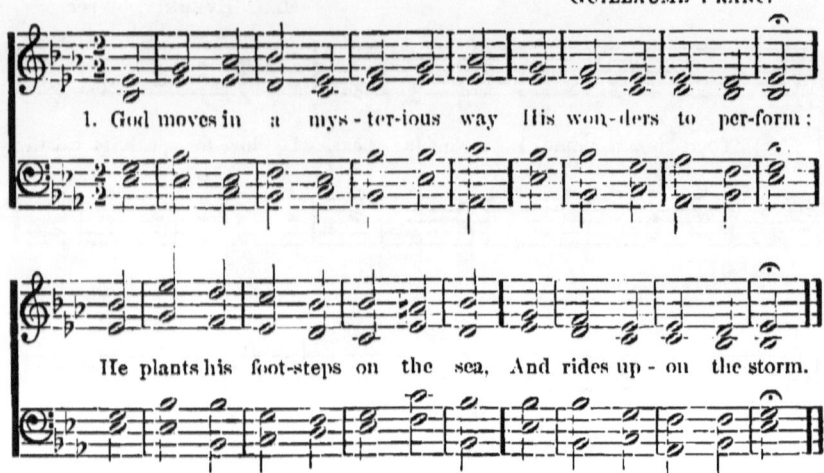

1. God moves in a mys-ter-ious way His won-ders to per-form;
He plants his foot-steps on the sea, And rides up-on the storm.

2 Deep in unfathomable mines
  Of never-failing skill
He treasures up his bright designs,
  And works his gracious will.

3 You fearful saints, fresh courage take;
  The clouds you so much dread
Are big with mercy, and shall break
  In blessings on your head.

4 Judge not the Lord by feeble sense,
  But trust him for his grace;
Behind a frowning providence
  He hides a smiling face.

5 His purposes will ripen fast,
  Unfolding every hour:
The bud may have a bitter taste,
  But sweet will be the flower.

6 Blind unbelief is sure to err,
  And scan his work in vain;
God is his own interpreter,
  And he will make it plain.

No. 190. C. M.

1 Thy kingdom, Lord, forever stands,
  While earthly thrones decay;
And time submits to thy commands,
  While ages roll away.

2 Thy sovereign bounty freely gives
  Its unexhausted store;
And universal nature lives
  On thy sustaining power.

3 Holy and just in all thy ways,
  Thy providence divine;

In all thy works, immortal rays
  Of power and mercy shine.

4 The praise of God—delightful theme!—
  Shall fill my heart and tongue;
Let all creation bless his name
  In one eternal song.

No. 191. C. M.

1 O God, our help in ages past,
  Our hope for years to come,
Our shelter from the stormy blast,
  And our eternal home!

2 Beneath the shadow of thy throne
  Thy saints have dwelt secure;
Sufficient is thine arm, alone,
  And our defense is sure.

3 Before the hills in order stood,
  Or earth received her frame,
From everlasting thou art God,
  To endless years the same.

4 A thousand ages in thy sight
  Are like an evening gone,
Short as the watch that ends the night
  Before the rising sun.

5 Time, like an ever-rolling stream,
  Bears all its sons away;
They fly, forgotten, as a dream
  Dies at the opening day.

6 O God, our help in ages past,
  Our hope for years to come,
Be thou our guard while life shall last,
  And our eternal home!

No. 192. HERMON. C. M.

JOHN P. McFERRIN, by per.

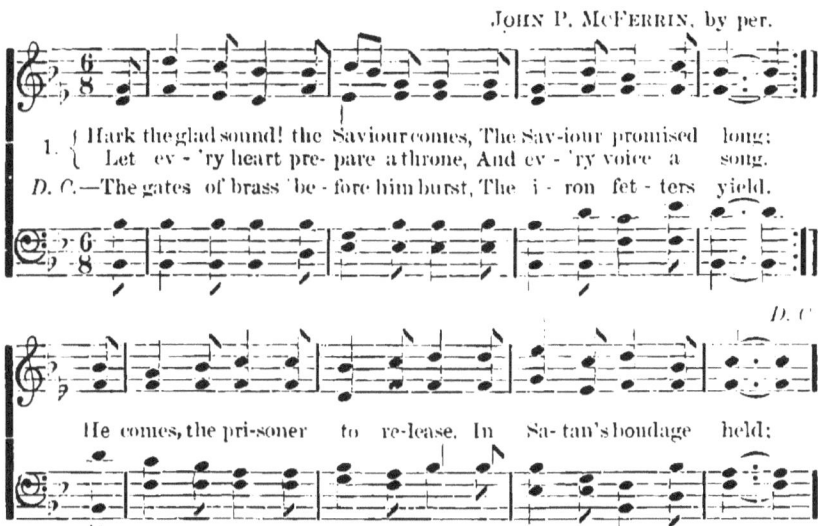

2 He comes, from thickest films of vice
  To clear the mental ray,
  And on the eyeballs of the blind
  To pour celestial day.

He comes, the broken heart to bind,
  The bleeding soul to cure,
And, with the treasures of his grace,
  T' enrich the humble poor.

No. 193. BROWN. C. M.

WM. B. BRADBURY.

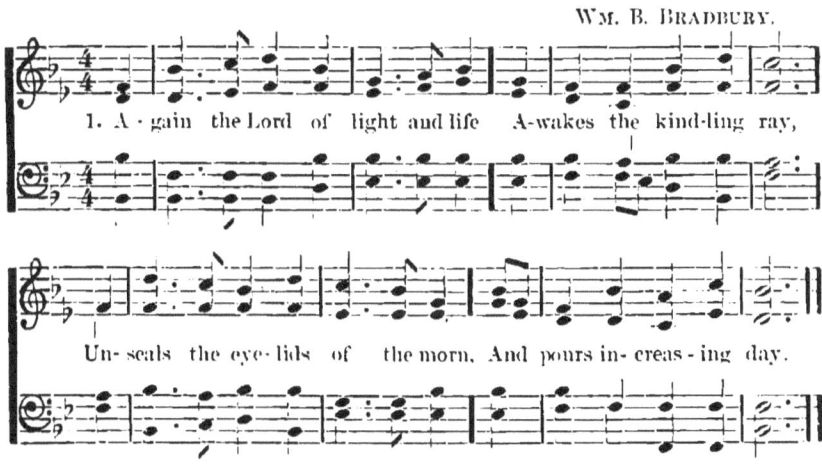

2 O what a night was that which wrapt
  The heathen world in gloom!
  O what a Sun which rose this day
  Triumphant from the tomb!

3 This day be grateful homage paid,
  And loud hosannas sung;

Let gladness dwell in every heart,
  And praise on every tongue.

4 Ten thousand different lips shall join
  To hail this welcome morn,
  Which scatters blessings from its wings
  To nations yet unborn.

No. 194. CORONATION. C. M.

1. All hail the pow'r of Jesus' name! Let angels prostrate fall: Bring forth the royal diadem, And crown him Lord of all: Bring forth the royal diadem, And crown him Lord of all.

2 Ye chosen seed of Israel's race,—
   A remnant weak and small,—
Hail him, who saves you by his grace,
   And crown him Lord of all.

3 Ye Gentile sinners, ne'er forget
   The wormwood and the gall:
Go, spread your trophies at his feet,
   And crown him Lord of all.

4 Let every kindred, every tribe
   On this terrestrial ball,
To him all majesty ascribe,
   And crown him Lord of all.

5 O that, with yonder sacred throng,
   We at his feet may fall,
We'll join the everlasting song,
   And crown him Lord of all.

No. 195. C. M.

1 Our souls are in the Saviour's hand,
   And he will keep them still;
And you and I shall surely stand
   With him on Zion's hill.

2 Him eye to eye we there shall see,
   Our face like his shall shine;
O what a glorious company,
   When saints and angels join!

3 O what a joyful meeting there,
   In robes of white array!
Palms in our hands we all shall bear,
   And crowns that ne'er decay.

4 When we've been there ten thousand years,
   Bright shining as the sun,
We've no less days to sing God's praise
   Than when we first begun!

No. 196. C. M.

1 O happy they who know the Lord,
   With whom he deigns to dwell!
He feeds and cheers them by his word,
   His arm supports them well.

2 To them, in each distressing hour,
   His throne of grace is near;
And when they plead his love and power,
   He stands engaged to hear.

3 His presence sweetens all our cares,
   And makes our burdens light;
A word from him dispels our fears,
   And gilds the gloom of night.

4 May we enjoy and highly prize
   These tokens of thy love,
Till thou shalt bid our spirits rise
   To worship thee above.

No. 197. ROWLEY. 5s, 6s & 9s.

LOWELL MASON.

1. How happy are they Who the Saviour o-bey, And have laid up their treasures a-bove! Tongue can-not ex-press The sweet com-fort and peace Of a soul in its ear-li-est love, Of a soul in its ear-li-est love.

2 This comfort is mine,
Since the favor divine
I have found in the blood of the Lamb.
Since the truth I believed,
What a joy I've received,
What a heaven in Jesus' blest name!

3 'Tis a heaven below
My Redeemer to know;
And the angels can do nothing more
Than to fall at his feet,
And the story repeat,
And the Lover of sinners adore.

4 Jesus all the day long
Is my joy and my song:
O that all to this refuge may fly!
He has loved me, I cried;
He has suffered and died
To redeem such a rebel as I!

5 On the wings of his love
I am carried above
All my sin and temptation and pain:

O why should I grieve,
While on him I believe?
O why should I sorrow again?

6 O the rapturous height
Of that holy delight,
Which I find in the life-giving blood!
Of my Saviour possessed,
I am perfectly blessed,
Being filled with the fullness of God!

7 Now my remnant of days
Will I spend to his praise,
Who has died, me from sin to redeem;
Whether many or few,
All my years are his due—
They shall all be devoted to him.

8 What a mercy is this!
What a heaven of bliss!
How unspeakably happy am I!
Gathered into the fold,
With believers enrolled—
With believers to live and to die!

No. 199. SCHUMANN. S. M.

L. C. EVERETT.

1. The Lord my Shep-herd is, I shall be well sup-plied: Since he is mine, and I am his, What can I want be-side! What can I want be-side?

2 He leads me to the place
　Where heavenly pasture grows,
　Where loving waters gently pass,
　And full salvation flows.

3 If e'er I go astray,
　He doth my soul reclaim,
　And guides me in his own right way,
　For his most holy name.

4 While he affords his aid,
　I cannot yield to fear; [shade,
　Tho' I should walk thro' death's dark
　My Shepherd's with me there.

No. 200. S. M.

1 O bless the Lord, my soul!
　His mercies bear in mind;
　Forget not all his benefits;
　The Lord to thee is kind.

2 He will not always chide;
　He will with patience wait;
　His wrath is ever slow to rise,
　And ready to abate.

3 He pardons all thy sins,
　Prolongs thy feeble breath;
　He healeth thine infirmities,
　And ransoms thee from death.

4 Then bless his holy name,
　Whose grace hath made thee whole,
　Whose loving-kindness crowns thy days:
　O bless the Lord, my soul!

No. 201. S. M.

1 How charming is the place
　Where my Redeemer, God,
　Unvails the beauties of his face,
　And sheds his love abroad!

2 Not the fair palaces
　To which the great resort
　Are once to be compared with this,
　Where Jesus holds his court.

3 Here, on the mercy-seat,
　With radiant glory crowned,
　Our joyful eyes behold him sit,
　And smile on all around.

4 To him their prayers and cries
　Each humble soul presents;
　He listens to their broken sighs,
　And grants them all their wants.

5 Give me, O Lord, a place
　Within thy blest abode,
　Among the children of thy grace,
　The servants of my God.

No. 202. BEALOTH. S. M. D.

Anon.

1. I love thy kingdom, Lord, The house of thine abode,
The Church our blest Redeemer saved With his own precious blood;
I love thy church, O God. Her walls before thee stand,
Dear as the apple of thine eye, And graven on thy hand.

2 For her my tears shall fall,
   For her my prayers ascend;
To her my cares and toils be given,
   Till toils and cares shall end.
Beyond my highest joy,
   I prize her heavenly ways,
Her sweet communion, solemn vows,
   Her hymns of love and praise.

3 Jesus, thou Friend divine,
   Our Saviour and our King,
Thy hand from every snare and foe
   Shall great deliverance bring.
Sure as thy truth shall last,
   To Zion shall be given
The brightest glories earth can yield,
   And brighter bliss of heaven.

No. 203. L. M.

1 Come to the house of prayer,
   O thou afflicted, come:
The God of peace shall meet thee there;
   He makes that house his home.

2 Come to the house of praise,
   Ye who are happy now;
In sweet accord your voices raise,
   In kindred homage bow.

3 Thou, whose benignant eye
   In mercy looks on all—
Who seest the tear of misery,
   And hear'st the mourner's call—

4 Up to thy dwelling-place
   Bear our frail spirits on,
Till they outstrip time's tardy pace,
   And heaven on earth be won.

No. 204. BOYLSTON. S. M.

Lowell Mason.

1. Not all the blood of beasts, On Jew-ish al-tars slain,

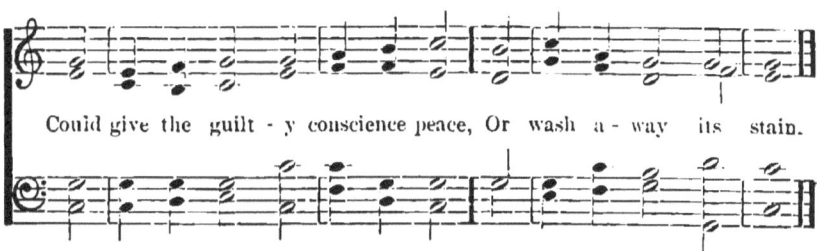

Could give the guilt-y conscience peace, Or wash a-way its stain.

2 But Christ, the heavenly Lamb,
  Bears all our sins away;
A sacrifice of nobler name
  And richer blood than they.

3 My faith would lay her hand
  On that dear head of thine,
While, like a penitent, I stand,
  And there confess my sin.

4 Believing, we rejoice
  To see the curse remove;
We bless the Lamb with cheerful voice,
  And sing his dying love.

No. 205. S. M.

1 Hungry, and faint, and poor,
  Behold us, Lord, again
Assembled at thy mercy's door,
  Thy bounty to obtain.

2 Thy word invites us nigh,
  Or we would starve indeed;
For we no money have to buy,
  Nor righteousness to plead.

3 The food our spirits want,
  Thy hand alone can give;
O hear the prayer of faith, and grant
  That we may eat and live!

No. 206. S. M.

1 Jesus invites his saints
  To meet around his board;
Here pardoned rebels sit, and hold
  Communion with their Lord.

2 This holy bread and wine
  Maintain our fainting breath,
By union with our living Lord,
  And interest in his death.

3 Let all our powers be joined
  His glorious name to raise;
Let holy love fill every mind,
  And every voice be praise.

No. 207. S. M.

1 Now is th' accepted time,
  Now is the day of grace;
Now, sinners, come, without delay,
  And seek the Saviour's face.

2 Now is th' accepted time,
  The Saviour calls to-day;
To-morrow it may be too late;
  Then why should you delay?

3 Now is th' accepted time,
  The gospel bids you come;
And every promise in his word
  Declares there yet is room.

No. 208. LABAN. S. M.

Geo. Heath. — Dr. L. Mason.

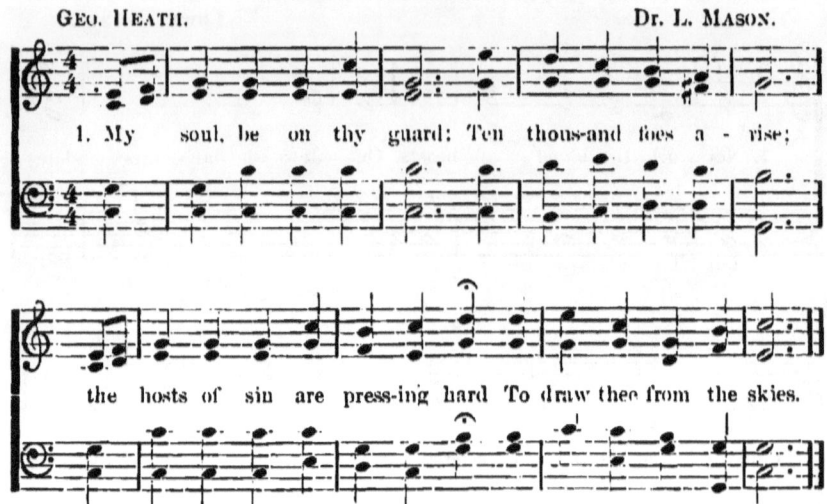

1. My soul, be on thy guard: Ten thousand foes arise; the hosts of sin are pressing hard To draw thee from the skies.

2 O watch, and fight, and pray;
 The battle ne'er give o'er;
 Renew it boldly every day,
 And help divine implore.

3 Ne'er think the victory won,
 Nor lay thine armor down;
 Thy arduous work will not be done
 Till thou obtain thy crown.

4 Fight on, my soul, till death
 Shall bring thee to thy God;
 He'll take thee, at thy parting breath,
 To his divine abode.

No. 209. S. M.

1 The Lord Jehovah reigns:
 Let all the nations fear;
 Let sinners tremble at his throne,
 And saints be humble there.

2 Jesus, the Saviour, reigns;
 Let earth adore its Lord;
 Bright cherubs his attendants wait,
 Swift to fulfill his word.

3 In Zion stands his throne;
 His honors are divine;
 His Church shall make his wonders known,
 For there his glories shine.

4 How holy is his name!
 How fearful is his praise!
 Justice, and truth, and judgment join
 In all the works of grace.

No. 210. S. M.

1 Blest be the tie that binds
 Our hearts in Christian love;
 The fellowship of kindred minds
 Is like to that above.

2 Before our Father's throne
 We pour our ardent prayers;
 Our fears, our hopes, our aims are one
 Our comforts and our cares.

3 We share our mutual woes,
 Our mutual burdens bear;
 And often for each other flows
 The sympathizing tear.

4 Here we must often part,
 In sorrow and in pain;
 But we shall still be joined in heart,
 And hope to meet again.

5 This glorious hope revives
 Our courage by the way;
 While each in expectation lives,
 And longs to see the day.

6 From sorrow, toil, and pain,
 And sin we shall be free;
 And perfect love and friendship reign
 Through all eternity.

No. 211. MOULTON. S. M.

L. C. CHISHOLM, by per.

1. Come, we who love the Lord, And let our joys be known;

Join in a song of sweet ac-cord, And thus sur-round the throne.

2 Let those refuse to sing
　Who never knew our God;
But children of the heavenly King
　May speak their joys abroad.

3 The men of grace have found
　Glory begun below;
Celestial fruits on earthly ground
　From faith and hope may grow.

4 The hill of Zion yields
　A thousand sacred sweets,
Before we reach the heavenly fields,
Or walk the golden streets.

5 Then let our songs abound,
　And every tear be dry;
We're marching through Immanuel's ground
To fairer worlds on high.

No. 212. S. M.

1 How honored is the place
　Where we adoring stand—
Zion, the glory of the earth,
　And beauty of the land!

2 Bulwarks of grace defend
　The city where we dwell;
While walls, of strong salvation made,
Defy th' assaults of hell.

3 Lift up th' eternal gates,
　The doors wide open fling;
Enter, ye nations, that obey
　The statutes of our King.

4 Here taste unmingled joys,
　And live in perfect peace,
You that have known Jehovah's name,
　And ventured on his grace.

No. 213. S. M.

1 Once more, before we part,
　O bless the Saviour's name!
Let every tongue and every heart
　Adore and praise the same.

2 Lord, in thy grace we came,
　That blessing still impart;
We met in Jesus' sacred name,
　In Jesus' name we part.

3 Still on thy holy word
　Help us to feed, and grow,
Still to go on to know the Lord,
　And practice what we know.

4 Now, Lord, before we part,
　Help us to bless thy name;
Let every tongue and every heart
　Adore and praise the same.

No. 214. OLIVET. 6s & 4s.

LOWELL MASON.

1. My faith looks up to thee, Thou Lamb of Cal-va-ry, Sav-iour di-vine;
{ Now hear me while I pray; } { Take all my guilt a-way; } O let me, from this day, Be whol-ly thine.

2 May thy rich grace impart
Strength to my fainting heart,
My zeal inspire;
As thou hast died for me,
O may my love to thee
Pure, warm, and changeless be—
A living fire.

3 While life's dark maze I tread,
And griefs around me spread,
Be thou my guide;

Bid darkness turn to day,
Wipe sorrow's tears away,
Nor let me ever stray
From thee aside.

4 When ends life's transient dream,
When death's cold, sullen stream
Shall o'er me roll,
Blest Saviour, then, in love,
Fear and distress remove;
O bear me safe above—
A ransomed soul.

No. 215. COOKHAM. 7s.

Arr. by R. M. McIntosh.

1. Sin-ners, turn—why will you die? God, your Mak-er, asks you why;
God, who did your be-ing give, Made you with him-self to live.

2 Sinners, turn—why will you die?
Christ, your Saviour, asks you why—
He who did your souls retrieve,
He who died that you might live.

3 Will you let him die in vain?
Crucify your Lord again?
Why, you ransomed sinners, why
Will you slight his grace and die?

4 Will you not his grace receive?
Will you still refuse to live?
O you dying sinners, why—
Why will you forever die?

No. 216. 7s.

1 'Tis religion that can give
Sweetest pleasure while we live;
'Tis religion must supply
Solid comfort when we die.

2 After death, its joys will be
Lasting as eternity;
Be the living God my friend,
Then my bliss shall never end.

No. 217. MARTYN. 7s. Double.

1. Je-sus, lov-er of my soul, Let me to thy bo-som fly.
   While the near-er wa-ters roll, While the tempest still is high;
D.C.—Safe in-to the ha-ven guide, O re-ceive my soul at last!

Hide me, O my Sav-iour, hide, Till the storm of life is past:

2 Other refuge have I none,
 Hangs my helpless soul on thee:
 Leave, ah! leave me not alone,
 Still support and comfort me!
 All my trust on thee is stayed,
 All my help from thee I bring,
 Cover my defenceless head
 With the shadow of thy wing.

3 Thou, O Christ, art all I want:
 More than all in thee I find:
 Raise the fallen, cheer the faint,
 Heal the sick, and lead the blind;

Just and holy is thy name;
 Prince of peace and righteousness:
 Most unworthy, Lord, I am;
 Thou art full of truth and grace.

4 Plenteous grace with thee is found,
 Grace to cover all my sin:
 Let the healing streams abound,
 Make and keep me pure within:
 Thou of life the fountain art;
 Freely let me take of thee:
 Spring thou up within my heart,
 Rise to all eternity!

No. 218. NETTLETON. 8s & 7s.

R. ROBINSON. Anon.

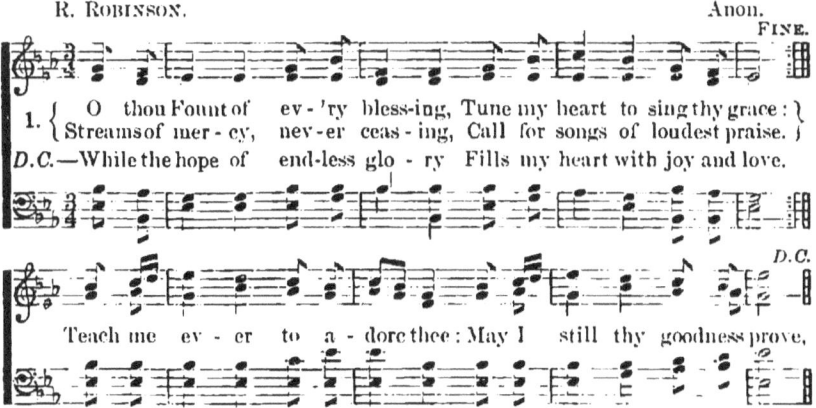

1. O thou Fount of ev-'ry bless-ing, Tune my heart to sing thy grace:
   Streams of mer-cy, nev-er ceas-ing, Call for songs of loudest praise.
D.C.—While the hope of end-less glo-ry Fills my heart with joy and love.

Teach me ev-er to a-dore thee: May I still thy goodness prove,

2 Here I'll raise my Ebenezer:
 Hither by thy help I've come;
 And I hope, by thy good pleasure,
 Safely to arrive at home.
 Jesus sought me when a stranger,
 Wandering from thy fold, O God;
 He, to rescue me from danger,
 Interposed his precious blood.

3 O to grace how great a debtor
 Daily I'm constrained to be!
 Let thy goodness, like a fetter,
 Bind me closer still to thee.
 Never let me wander from thee,
 Never leave thee, whom I love;
 By thy Word and Spirit guide me,
 Till I reach thy courts above.

No. 219. ROCK OF AGES. 7s. 6 lines.

1. Rock of ages, cleft for me, Let me hide my-self in thee:
D.C.—Be of sin the dou-ble cure, Save from wrath and make me pure.

Let the wa - ter and the blood, From thy wounded side which flowed,

2 Could my tears forever flow,
Could my zeal no languor know,
These for sin could not atone;
Thou must save, and thou alone;
In my hand no price I bring,
Simply to thy cross I cling.

3 While I draw this fleeting breath,
When my eyes shall close in death,
When I rise to worlds unknown,
And behold thee on thy throne,
Rock of ages, cleft for me,
Let me hide myself in thee.

No. 220. FARMVILLE.

CHARLOTTE ELLIOT. R. M. McINTOSH, by per.

1. Just as I am without one plea, But that thy blood was shed for me, And that thou bidst me come to thee—O Lamb of God, I come! O Lamb of God, I come!

2 Just as I am—and waiting not
To rid my soul of one dark blot,[spot:
To thee, whose blood can cleanse each
‖: O Lamb of God, I come! :‖

3 Just as I am—though tossed about
With many a conflict, many a doubt,
With fears within and wars without—
‖: O Lamb of God, I come! :‖

4 Just as I am—poor, wretched, blind:
Sight, riches, healing of the mind,
Yea, all I need, in thee to find,
‖: O Lamb of God, I come! :‖

5 Just as I am—thy love unknown
Has broken every barrier down;
Now to be thine, yea, thine alone,
‖: O Lamb of God, I come! :‖

No. 221. SABBATH. 7s. Double.

LOWELL MASON.

1. Safely through another week, God has brought us on our way;
Let us now a blessing seek; Waiting in his courts to-day.
Day of all the week the best, Emblem of eternal rest;
Day of all the week the best, Emblem of eternal rest.

2 While we seek supplies of grace,
   Through the dear Redeemer's name,
Show thy reconciling face—
   Take away our sin and shame;
From our worldly cares set free,
May we rest this day in thee.

3 Here we come thy name to praise;
   Let us feel thy presence near;
May thy glory meet our eyes,
   While we in thy house appear:
Here afford us, Lord, a taste
Of our everlasting feast.

4 May the gospel's joyful sound
   Conquer sinners, comfort saints,
Make the fruits of grace abound,
   Bring relief from all complaints:
Thus let all our Sabbaths prove,
Till we join the Church above.

OH! THE GOOD WE ALL MAY DO. Concluded.

Je - - sus we are true, Oh! the good we all may do.
If to Je- sus we are true, we are true.

No. 223. ZION. 8s, 7s & 4s.

Dr. Thos. Hastings.

1 { On the mountain's top ap-pear-ing, Lo, the sa-cred her-ald stands,
{ Wel-come news to Zi-on bear-ing, Zi-on long in hos-tile lands:

Verse.

Mourn-ing cap-tive, God him-self shall loose thy bands.

Chorus.

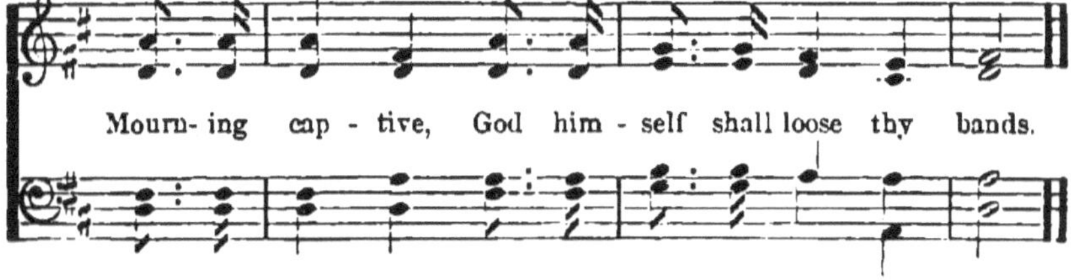

Mourn-ing cap-tive, God him-self shall loose thy bands.

2 Has thy night been long and mournful,
All thy friends unfaithful proved?
Have thy foes been proud and scornful,
By thy sighs and tears unmoved?
Cease thy mourning.
Zion still is well beloved.

3 God, thy God, will now restore thee!
He himself appears thy friend:
All thy foes shall flee before thee,
Here their boasts and triumphs end
Great deliverance.
Zion's King vouchsafes to send.

No. 224. I LOVE TO TELL THE STORY.

KATE HANKEY. WM. G. FISCHER, by per.

1. I love to tell the story Of unseen things above, Of Jesus and his glory, Of Jesus and his love. I love to tell the story Because I know 'tis true: It satisfies my longings As nothing else can do.

2. I love to tell the story; More wonderful it seems Than all the golden fancies Of all our golden dreams. I love to tell the story It did so much for me! And that is just the reason I tell it now to thee.

CHORUS.
I love to tell the story, 'Twill be my theme in glory, To tell the old, old story, Of Jesus and his love.

3 I love to tell the story;
'Tis pleasant to repeat
What seems each time I tell it,
More wonderfully sweet.
I love to tell the story;
For some have never heard
The message of salvation
From God's own holy word.

4 I love to tell the story;
For those who know it best
Seem hungering and thirsting
To hear it like the rest.
And when, in scenes of glory,
I sing the new, new song,
'Twill be—the old, old story
That I have loved so long.

No. 225. GREENVILLE. 8. 7. Double.

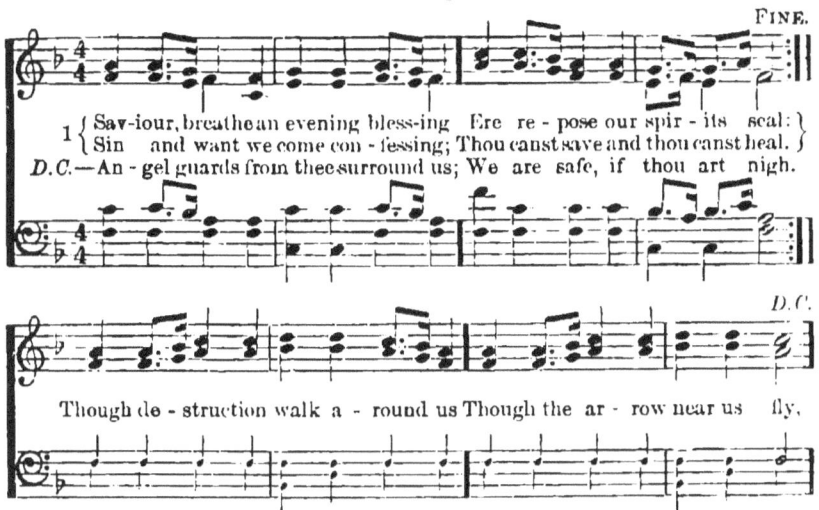

1 { Sav-iour, breathe an evening bless-ing Ere re-pose our spir-its seal:
  { Sin and want we come con-fessing; Thou canst save and thou canst heal. }
D.C.—An-gel guards from thee surround us; We are safe, if thou art nigh.

Though de-struction walk a-round us Though the ar-row near us fly,

2 Though the night be dark and dreary,
  Darkness cannot hide from thee;
  Thou art he who, never weary,
  Watcheth where thy people be.

Should swift death this night o'ertake us,
And our couch become our tomb,
May the morn in heaven awake us,
Clad in light, and deathless bloom.

No. 226. C. M.

1 Dismiss us with thy blessing, Lord;
  Help us to feed upon thy word;
  All that has been amiss, forgive,
  And let thy truth within us live.

2 Though we are guilty, thou art good;
  Cleanse all our sins in Jesus' blood.
  Give every burdened soul release,
  And bid us all depart in peace,

No. 227. PRAISE GOD.

Praise God, from whom all blessing flow; Praise him, all creatures here below;

Praise him above, ye heavenly host; Praise Father, Son, and Ho-ly Ghost.

No. 228. DEAL GENTLY, O FATHER.

Copyright, 1891, by R. M. McIntosh.

DEAL GENTLY, O FATHER. Concluded.

No. 229. COME UNTO ME.

R. M. McIntosh, by per.

Copyright, 1891, by R. M. McIntosh.

COME UNTO ME. Concluded.

207

No. 230. How Lovely are Thy Dwellings.

R. M. McIntosh, by per.

How Lovely are Thy Dwellings. Concluded.

14 R N   209

No. 231. MY SHEEP HEAR MY VOICE.

R. M. McIntosh, by per.

MY SHEEP HEAR MY VOICE. Continued.

No. 232. IN MY FATHER'S HOUSE.

IN MY FATHER'S HOUSE. Concluded.

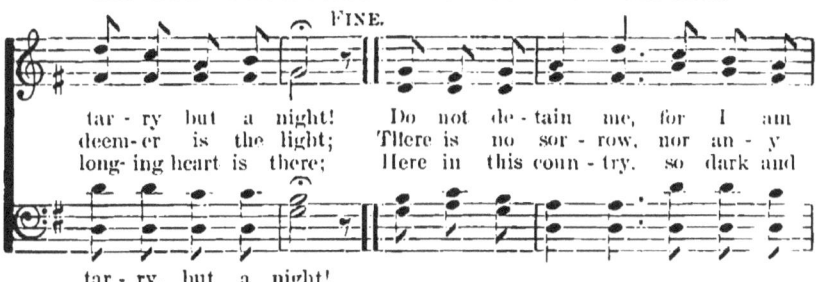

No. 233. WILMOT. 7s.

C. M. von WEBER.

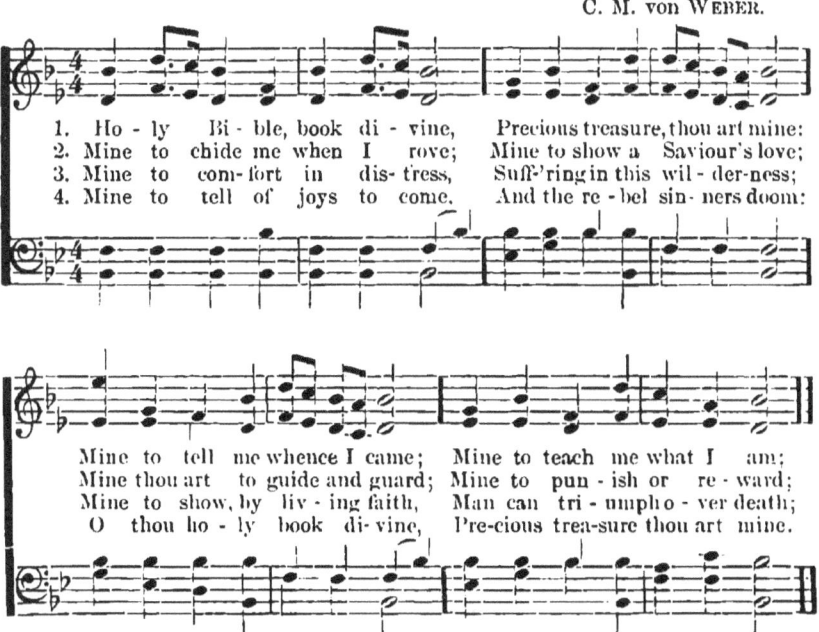

1. Ho-ly Bi-ble, book di-vine, Precious treasure, thou art mine:
2. Mine to chide me when I rove; Mine to show a Saviour's love;
3. Mine to com-fort in dis-tress, Suff'ring in this wil-der-ness;
4. Mine to tell of joys to come, And the re-bel sin-ners doom:

Mine to tell me whence I came; Mine to teach me what I am;
Mine thou art to guide and guard; Mine to pun-ish or re-ward;
Mine to show, by liv-ing faith, Man can tri-umph o-ver death;
O thou ho-ly book di-vine, Pre-cious trea-sure thou art mine.

No. 234. "I WAS GLAD."

"I WAS GLAD." Continued.

"I WAS GLAD." Concluded.

INDEX OF TITLES AND FIRST LINES.

A

	NO.		NO.
A charge to keep I have	47	Bethany.	134
Again the Lord of light and life	193	Beyond the cares of life and bitter	108
A heritage of splendor free	27	Bless us and keep us.	62
A little longer labor on	67	Blest be the tie that binds	210
All hail the power of Jesus' name	194	Bonnell. C. M.	72
Amazing grace! how sweet the	174	Boylston. S. M.	204
Anthem. Arise, Shine; for thy	146	Bringing in the sheaves.	106
Antioch. C. M.	76	Broker. L. M.	95
Are there few that be saved?	7	Brown. C. M.	193
Ariel.	81	Buried beneath the yielding wave	184
Arise, arise, shine, shine;	146	By and by all this weeping and	115
Arlington. C. M.	155	By faith we find the place above	10
Art thou tempted and tried?	69		
As doves to their windows.	107	## C	
Ashville. C. M.	138	Calling thee away.	108
Asleep in Jesus! blessed sleep	152	Chiefest among ten thousand.	97
At the fount of love.	94	Children's hymn	89
Avon. C. M.	184	Children of Jerusalem.	28
Awake, and sing the song of	68	Christmas. C. M.	176
Awake! awake! the master now	142	Christ, the Lord, is risen to-day	124
Awake, my soul stretch every	176	Church rallying song	142
Azmon. C. M.	132	Come and drink to-day.	94
## B		Come, humble sinner in whose	170
Balerma. C. M.	179	Come, let us a-new	198
Bealoth. S. M. D.	202	Come, let us join.	178
Beautiful Zion	5	Come, sinner, to the gospel.	140
Be content with your lot.	29	Come to-day	60
Before Jehovah's awful throne.	148	Come to me.	25
Behold a stranger at the door	143	Come to Jesus, come to Jesus	126
Behold the amazing sight	43	Come to Jesus just now.	126
Behold the lamb	44	Come to the house.	203
Be it my only wisdom	33	Come to the father's house.	122
Be of good courage	75	Come unto me	229

	No.
Come unto me, the Saviour said	116
Come weary souls, with sin	154
Come, we who love the Lord	211
Cookman. 7s.	215
Coronation. C. M.	194
Crichlow L. M.	87

D

	No.
Davies. 7s.	78
Deal Gently, O Father.	228
Dismiss us with thy blessing	226
Doggett. C. M.	169
Do you hear that gentle whisper?	59
Duke Street. L. M.	161
Duncan. S. M.	31
Dundee. C. M.	189

E

	No.
Enter in.	120

F

	No.
Fade, fade each earthly joy	41
Farmville	220
Father of love	51
Father of mercies.	118
Father whate'er of earthly bliss	171
From all that dwell below the	166
From every stormy wind that	150
From the sunny morning	89

G

	No.
Gathering in the harvest.	82
Gathering the harvest.	82
Georgia. S. M.	43
Gill. 8s, 7s & 4s.	24
God is calling you.	39
God moves in a mysterious way	189
God speed the right.	1
Gregory	33
Greenville. 8, 7 Double.	225
Guide me, O my blessed Saviour	135

H

	No.
Hallelujah.	36
Hallelujah! cease all mourning	36
Happy the home, when God is	159
Hark the glad sound the Saviour	192
Hark the herald angels sing	8

	No.
Harp. C. M.	174
Hear my voice entreating.	25
Hear the Master calling	16
Hear the Saviour's invitation.	60
Hear ye not the voice of Jesus?	120
Heavenly Father, keep me near	85
Heber. C. M.	168
Hebron. L. M.	162
He calleth me home	45
He is ever faithful.	80
Hermon. C. M.	192
Her sad vigil keeping	38
High in the heavens.	163
Hoge. L. M.	151
Holy bible, book divine.	233
Home. C. M.	157
Home and rest.	93
Home of our Father's love	114
Hosanna to our conquering king	160
How charming is the place	201
How happy are they who the	197
How honored is the place	212
How kind a friend is Jesus	48
How kind is the heart of the	117
How lovely are thy dwellings	230
How precious is the book divine	183
How sweet, how heavenly.	155
How sweet the name of Jesus	72
How sweet to be there.	104
How vain is all beneath the	151
Hungry, and faint, and poor	205

I

	No.
I am on my way to heaven	61
I heard the voice of Jesus say	79
I know a healing fountain	101
I know that my Redeemer. L. M.	153
I know that my Redeemer. C. M.	138
I lean on his wonderful might	125
I love thy kingdom Lord	202
I love to tell the story.	224
I'll be there.	56
I'm not ashamed to own my	132
I'm thinking of Jesus of glory	104
I never will leave thee.	66
In memory of the Saviour's love	172
In my Father's house	232

	NO.		NO.
In our Father's house	46	Let us with a joyful.	80
In our school again assembled	52	Little pilgrims	2
In the sweet by and by	115	Live for Jesus	90
Into the tent where a gypsy	86	Look away to Jesus.	119
Is thy heart defiled?	119	Loving Jesus, gentle lamb.	78
It is coming	4	Lucas. 10, 5s & 11s.	198
It is good to trust in Jesus.	110		
It will never grow old.	129		

M

I walk not alone	37	Majestic sweetness sits enthroned	130
I was glad	234	Manoah. C. M.	130
I will lead thee.	64	Many mansions.	23
		Many, many are the mansions.	23

J

		Martyn. 7s. Double	217
Jehovah reigns; he dwells	164	May God's blessing e'er attend you	32
Jesus! and shall it ever be	87	Mear. C. M.	180
Jesus, a true friend	48	Moulton. S. M.	211
Jesus, I love thy charming name	158	My heritage in heaven.	27
Jesus, I my cross have taken	112	My faith looks up to thee	214
Jesus in Gethsemane.	70	My sheep hear my voice.	231
Jesus, in the transporting name	188	My soul, be on thy guard	208
Jesus is mine.	41		

N

Jesus is passing by	96		
Jesus is passing the blind man	96	Naomi. C. M	171
Jesus, lover of my soul	217	Nearer, my God, to thee.	134
Jesus, the conqu'ror, reigns.	21	Nettleton. 8s & 7s.	218
Jesus, thou art the sinner's friend.	156	No sweeter song is heard on earth.	121
Jesus will let you in.	122	Not all the blood of beasts.	204
Jesus will receive thee.	109	Now is the accepted time	207
Jesus invites his saints	208	Now to heaven our prayers.	1
Joy to the world.	76		
Just as I am	220		

O

Just over the river	114	O bless the Lord, my soul	200
		O earnest toiler for the Lord	67

K

		O for a heart to praise my God	167
		O God of Bethel	180
Kavanaugh. L. M.	140	O God, our help in ages past	191
Keep me day by day.	19	O happy they who know the Lord	196
Keep me near thee	85	O have you not heard of that.	129
Keep me, Saviour, day by.	19	O how dear are the friendships	131
King Jesus, reign forevermore.	165	Oh! the good we all may do	222
		Oh, to be there.	20

L

		O Jesus! I never will leave thee	66
Laban. S. M.	208	O land of rest for thee I sigh	157
Lamp of our feet	65	Old Hundred. L. M.	148
Leave it to him.	102	Old Hundred. (Doxology.)	227
Leave me not, for I am lonely	103	O love divine.	81
Leave me not, O gentle Saviour.	103	Olivet. 6 & 4s.	214
Lebanon. 7s.	124	Once more before we part	213

	No.		No.
On the mountain's top appearing	223	Schumann. S. M.	199
On the way to heaven.	61	See him in the garden lone	70
Onward, dear pilgrim, faint and	64	Seek for the wanderers	145
Onward, still onward we're	10	Shall we know each other there?	14
Onward we're marching	40	Siloam. C. M.	173
Ortonville. C. M.	170	Sinners, turn, why will you	215
O think of his wonderful love	137	Since I can read my title clear	169
O thou fount of every blessing	218	Sitting at the feet of Jesus	57
O thou God of my salvation.	24	Solitude. C. M.	186
O thou who driest the mourner's	179	Songs in the heart	15
Our souls are in the Saviour's	195	Sowing in the morning.	106
Over the silent sea.	30	Sow in the morn	31
		Spring. C. M.	167
		Standing by the cross	73

P

Parting hymn.	32	Steadily marching on	141
Paul. S. M.	21	St. Thomas. S. M	68
Pilgrim. 8s & 7s.	99	Summers. L. M.	163
Pilgrim, thro' this barren land.	3	Sunshine and shadow	84
Pleading with thee.	139	Sweet the moments, rich in	73
Praise God from whom all	227		
Praise him.	18		
Praise ye the Lord	141		
Press on for the right	100		
Press Onward!	26		
Press onward, oh, Christian.	26		

T

Take my life, and let it be	12
Take your harps.	74
Tempted and tried.	69
Tell it again	86
That gentle whisper	59

R

Radiant clime of the pure.	20	The children for Jesus.	77
Raise aloft the standard	127	The feast is waiting.	35
Rally round the standard	100	The feast of love is waiting	35
Remember me	156	The golden gate	111
Rest. L. M.	152	The half he has never revealed	63
Rest to the weary soul.	83	The Lamb of Calvary.	53
Retreat. L. M.	150	The lessons are all about Jesus	133
Richmond. S. M. (Double.)	47	The Lord Jehovah reigns.	209
Rise, O my soul stretch every	177	The Lord my Shepherd is.	199
Rock of Ages.	219	The master calleth for thee.	38
Ross. C. M.	10	The master stood at the vineyard	95
Rowley. 5s, 6s & 9s.	197	The merciful Lord is my shepherd	125
		The Saviour is my all in all	144
		The stranger at the door.	143
		The sweetest song.	121

S

Sabbath. 7s. Double.	221	The vineyard gate.	96
Safely through another week.	221	The voice of Jesus.	79
Safely through another year.	62	The wonderful Saviour.	117
Saviour, breathe an evening	225	There's a call for willing workers	54
Saviour, guide me	135	There's a call for the willing.	54
Say, are few to be saved of men?	7	There's a great day coming	105

	NO.		NO.
There's a hand that's writing now	6	We sing thy praises, O Zion	5
There is a land immortal	123	What a friend we have in Jesus	147
There is a name I love to hear	186	What glory gilds the sacred page	182
There's a song of joy in our	15	What shall I render to my	175
There is a voice of the tenderest	139	What shall our record be?	6
There was love, deep love	53	When I survey the wondrous cross	161
They shall shine	71	When I walked with my God	84
They that wait upon the Lord	17	When languor and disease invade	185
Think gently of the erring one	173	When musing sorrow weeps the	49
Thou art the way, to thee	187	When shall we stand at yon portal	88
Though far from the fold	45	When the harvest all is in	58
Thus far the Lord, hath led	162	When the night comes on,	93
Thy kingdom, Lord, forever	190	When the roll is called	56
'Tis midnight and on Olive's brow	95	When we've crossed death's	14
'Tis religion that can give	216	Where are you going, oh,	13
To us a child of hope is born	128	Where the living waters flow	83
Truro. L. M.	149	Whither goest thou pilgrim	99
Trust him	3	Who is this that comes from	136
		Who shall abide?	91

U

		Why go around with troubled	102
Up to the work	11	Wilmot. 7s	233
		Will you come?	9

V

		With joyful hearts we sing	113
		With joy we meditate the grace	181
Vaughan. C. M.	185	With one consent let all the	149
Vile and sinful, though thou art	109	With sacred joy we lift our	168
Virginia	49	Woodland. C. M.	181
		Would you go home with the angels	13

W

		Would you stand among the toilers	58
Walk with me, gracious Lord	55		
We are coming	42		

Y

We are little pilgrims	2	Yarbrough	12
We are thy little lambs	92	Ye heralds of the cross	50
Weary watches for the morning	111	Ye friends of the blessed redeemer	145
We call thee	22	Yon portals fair	88
We'll gather the children of want	34		
We'll gather them in	34	## Z	
We praise him	52	Zion. 8s, 7s & 4s.	223
We shall meet again	131	Zerah. C. M.	128

THE J. M. ARMSTRONG COMPANY,
Music Typographers, Printers and Binders,
710 Sansom Street, Phila., Pa.

www.ingramcontent.com/pod-product-compliance
Lightning Source LLC
Chambersburg PA
CBHW021013240426
43669CB00037B/1085